Jerusalem

JERUSALEM

by
G. Frederick Owen

Introduction by Lowell Thomas

BEACON HILL PRESS OF KANSAS CITY
Kansas City, Missouri

6

Contents

ILLUSTRATION CREDITS:

Drawing of Herod's Temple on end sheets by Ken Butler and Jack D. Thompson under the direction of the author

Map of Jerusalem in New Testament Times by G. Frederick Owen and George Owen Holland

Photos by G. Eric Matson, pages 34, 71, 82, 93, 98, 103, 116, 119, 121, 124, 126, 129, 132, 134, 137, 151

Photos by W. Braun, pages 80, 145, 147, 149, 154, 162

Photos by David Harris, page 73; S. J. Schweig, page 101; Elia Photo Service, page 113; Israel Government Tourist Office, page 170 and front jacket

Jacket design by George Owen Holland

Introduction

When Ernest Renan wrote his still-popular *Life of Jesus,* he included a "fifth Gospel" among his authoritative sources. The first four Gospels were, of course, the writings of the Evangelists, Matthew, Mark, Luke, and John, as we find them in the New Testament. The "fifth Gospel" was Palestine itself.

Renan argued that no one could understand the origins of Christianity unless he took the trouble to familiarize himself with the Holy Land—the topography and terrain, the climate and wildlife, the cities and hamlets, wherein were played out those transcendent events that occurred during the reign of the Emperor Tiberias. Before describing the Sermon on the Mount, Renan would climb the hills of Galilee, re-creating in his imagination the scene where the Beatitudes were pronounced. Feeling the hot sunlight overhead, coughing as he kicked up dust underfoot, he mastered the locale, and gave a new kind of factual authenticity to his account of Christ's mission (whatever one may think of Renan's somewhat weak, rationalistic interpretation of that mission).

Today we know much more about the "fifth Gospel" than Renan or any other savant of the nineteenth century, however learned. Archaeologists have uncovered places so utterly lost since biblical times that their very existence used to be denied. Historians have correlated Palestinian cultures with those of Egypt, Mesopotamia, Iran, and Anatolia. The carbon-dating process has pinpointed chronologies with an accuracy never before possible. Information about the Holy Land becomes more detailed, systematic, and comprehensive every year.

Where this subject is concerned, research spills over the boundaries of strict, staid scholarship. No one can be cool, abstract, and disinterested about a land that is holy for three of the world's great religions: Judaiam, Christianity, Islam. Hence the loving care and profound veneration behind the search for its antiquities, and the conviction that they hold a unique significance for humanity. But antiquities are only part of the story in this quarter of the globe where time seems less real than anywhere else. The past merges into the present. The latest headlines mean no more, and often a lot less, than events that happened two or three millennia ago. Politicians and military men whom we can see in the flesh lack the persuasiveness of the prophets and the apostles.

That kind of thinking infuses this book, written by Dr. G. Frederick Owen, and illustrated chiefly by Mr. G. Eric Matson. It could hardly have been otherwise, since both of these men have lived and researched in that land so long, and now they focus their attention on the most sacred site of all—Jerusalem itself.

Their cooperation results in a guided tour through the ages. Here you will find tangible things that give substance to the Bible—Mount Moriah, where David brought the ark of the covenant; the conduit through which Hezekiah channeled water from Gihon Spring to the Pool of Siloam; the Mount of Olives, where Jesus taught His disciples; Gethsemane, scene of the Agony in the Garden. Here you will find the living reality associated with the Wailing Wall, the Church of the Holy Sepulchre, the Dome of the Rock. And in between, you will find references to the Canaanites, the Maccabees, the Crusaders, the Turks, the Israelis, and others who have held the City of David at one period or another during the rhythmic pulsations of Clio's pendulum across more than 3,000 years of human history.

A volume such as this invites each reader to turn to the pages on a subject that holds a particular interest for him. I turned first to the pages on Allenby's entrance into Jerusalem on December 11, 1917.

That moment stirred the nations of the West because the commanding general, Sir Edmund Allenby, had succeeded where Richard the Lion-hearted had failed eight centuries earlier at the time of the Third Crusade. It stirs me to this day for personal reasons. I happened to be in Jerusalem at this climax of the British campaign against the Turks, and was fortunate in getting acquainted with the great leader known as "the Bull" and his right arm just in from the desert, Lawrence of Arabia.

Ever since the defeat of the Crusaders by the Saracens under the knightly Saladin, Jerusalem had belonged to Islam. First came the Arabs, then the Seljuk Turks, and finally the Ottoman Turks, builders of the Ottoman Empire sprawling from the Balkans to Arabia. But by 1914 the Sultan sat on a shaky throne, which began to totter when he entered World War One on the side of the Central Powers. Allenby struck the blow that, setting up delayed reactions, knocked the throne over, knocked the Sultans into history, knocked the Turks out of their ramshackle empire into the modern state created by Kemal Ataturk.

All this followed from the liberation of Palestine. Shattering the enemy defense line at Beersheba, Allenby rolled the Turkish forces northward in a masterly campaign that took him past Jerusalem to Damascus and Aleppo. He entered the Holy City through the Jaffa Gate, on foot, without display of any kind—no martial music or triumphant banners—went directly to the Tower of David, and read his proclamation guaranteeing peace and freedom of worship to all peoples of all religions.

I noted the description of the Tower of David in this book with considerable interest. That was where the Duke of Connaught (the king's uncle) presented decorations to the military, following which ceremony I was invited to lunch with him and Allenby. Sir Ronald Storrs, the governor of Jerusalem, the "modern Pontius Pilate," had recently introduced me to Lawrence, so at lunch I had the sense, or maybe it was beginner's luck, to put in a few queries about T.E. As a result, Allenby okayed my trip to Arabia to visit the leader of the Revolt in the Desert. A day or two later "the Bull" invited me to the German hospice, mentioned in the pages that follow, where the Kaiser in his palmy days had had himself painted in rather illustrious, rather incongruous company, namely, Christ and the apostles. Here we sat for an hour or so, with Allenby's top generals, the Anglican bishop, and the Duke of Connaught. We were high up in the tower, where we had a superb view of the Holy City below us on one side, and the old Jericho Road, the Dead Sea, and the Hills of Moab to the east.

Having been back to Jerusalem many times, I could discourse at length about the extraordinary individuals I've met there. Aside from Allenby and Lawrence, number one, perhaps, would be Mrs. Bertha Vester, who in 1917 provided the mayor with a white sheet to use as a flag of surrender. Half of that flag is one of my prized possessions, as is my recollection of Mrs. Vester, a grand lady who for half a century was the most prominent American and the most indefatigable Good Samaritan in the city.

The tendency to go on and on must be resisted. After all, the business of an introduction is to introduce. So, having given you a prologue to the action, I'll step aside and let Dr. Owen take you to Jerusalem.

—LOWELL THOMAS

Thus saith the Lord God unto Jerusalem;

Thy birth and thy nativity is of the land of Canaan; thy father was an Amorite, and thy mother an Hittite. . . . in the day thou wast born thy navel was not cut, neither wast thou washed in water . . . thou wast not salted . . . nor swaddled at all. . . .

When I passed by thee, and saw thee . . . I said . . . Live. . . . I spread my skirt over thee, and covered thy nakedness: yea, I sware unto thee, and entered into a covenant with thee, saith the Lord God, and thou becamest mine.

Then washed I thee with water . . . and I anointed thee with oil. I clothed thee also with broidered work, and shod thee . . . and I girded thee about with fine linen, and I covered thee with silk. . . . and thou wast exceeding beautiful, and didst prosper into a kingdom.

—Ezek. 16:3-13

When God created beauty, He created 10 parts of it and gave nine to Jerusalem; when He created knowledge, He did the same; and the same when He created suffering.

CHAPTER 1

The History of Jerusalem

In the wild pasturelands of the Judean mountains, far removed from the usual runways of men, lies <u>Jerusalem, "the City of Peace</u>." God set her "in the midst of the nations"[1] and gave her such a place in the affections of men that the very name awakens sacred memories and stirs the soul more deeply than the mention of any other city of the world.

Jerusalem's unparalleled past with regard to her 13

splendid temples, her comfortable palaces, and the rich color and glow of her abounding wealth are gone. Yet there are elements that do not change. Her contribution to humanity is immeasurable, and her exalted line of moral and spiritual truth remains. Her form and outline are there, and her relation to the landscape and to the land are unchanged. The past reasserts itself, even in the midst of the commotions of the present.

She is yet, and always will be, in moral form, one of the loftiest plateaus of the world, "exalted in the imagination and memory of Jews and Christians and Mohammedans—a metropolis of infinite human hopes and longings and devotions." Hither come innumerable companies of men and women from every country and clime weeping beside the wall of their vanished Temple, seeking the place of the Crucifixion, or desiring to pray where Moslem tradition says Mohammed prayed. Century after century these human throngs have toiled upward to this ancient city where the ever-changing winds from the desert and the sea sweep and shift over the rocky hilltops, the mute gray battlements, and the domes crowned with the Star of David, the cross of Christ, and the crescent of Mohammed. Thither will the attention of millions be turned who cannot but would like to come.

Almost all of the great cities of the world have been located on rivers or near important waterways. Some have stood at the crossroads of world commerce. All have grown great by agriculture, art, education, commerce, industry, or finance. Only Jerusalem is different. It has no river; it is near no waterway, and has ever been removed from the main crossroads of world commerce; yet it abides while most other great cities of antiquity have passed away.

Through the prophet Ahijah, God spoke of Jerusalem as "the city which I have chosen me to put my name there."[2] And through Isaiah, He promised to be unto Jerusalem "a place of broad rivers and streams; wherein shall go no galley with oars, neither shall gallant ship pass thereby."[3] And for long centuries His presence seems to have been so connected with the city that there has been a mystic sublimity and perpetual vigor which have caused historians to regard it as the greatest earthly marvel known to men.

This far-famed city, whose influence has often inspired and transformed other cities, began as a settlement about 3000 B.C., according to generally accepted archaeological evidence. It first appeared in written records some 4,000 years ago as a chief city of the ancient Canaanites. Since 1400 B.C., Jerusalem has appeared in an important role within almost every generation of men which has come and gone. It has been the focal point of so many hopes that the place holds a fascination for the minds of men as no other city on the face of the earth.

Some 18 centuries before Christ, Abraham returned from his successful expedition against the kings "of the nations" and paid tithes to Melchizedek, "king of Salem" and "priest of the most high God."[4] Four hundred twenty-five years later "Uru-Salem" was repeatedly mentioned in the *Tell el-Amarna* tablets as Abdi-Heba, the governor of *Uru-Salem,* wrote letters to Amenhotep III and his son Amenhotep IV (Pharaoh Akhenaton), of Egypt. He stated that Palestine was being overrun by the "Habiru" (the Hebrews, as some think), and that Jerusalem would soon be taken unless Egyptian troops were sent to defend the city.[5]

As the Hebrew conquest under Joshua progressed, the king of Jerusalem joined with the kings of Hebron, Jarmuth, Lachish, and Eglon in a confederacy against the Israelites.[6] Under Joshua the Israelites fought against Jerusalem and smote it "with the edge of the sword, and set the city on fire." Joshua then assigned it to the tribe of Benjamin, but they permitted the government of the city to remain in the hands of the Jebusites. Soon Jerusalem throne, cleansed the Temple, and restored the solemn rites. He reinstated the Levites, demolished the false gods, removed the groves, threw down the high places, and destroyed the brazen serpent which was being superstitiously worshipped in the Temple. Hezekiah also built the Siloam Tunnel, restored much of Jerusalem's grandeur, and withstood Sennacherib of Assyria (701 B.C.) until the angel of the Lord smote 185,000 of the invaders, and caused the king to return "with shame of face to his own land."[11]

But the irreligious and evil practices of Manasseh, Hezekiah's son and successor, ran riot and brought on a long moral drift which was checked only under King Josiah (641-610 B.C.). During his reign a deep religious concern swept Jerusalem and all the land, even reaching the northern kingdom of Israel. Prophets were born (Zephaniah, Nahum, Habakkuk, Jeremiah); the Temple was again cleansed. Hilkiah not only rediscovered the scroll of the sacred law in the Temple archives, but the king and the prophets read it to the people, who obeyed its authority and prospered in the way of righteousness.

But the revival or reformation lasted for only a few years, then subsided when King Josiah fell needlessly in the battle at the Pass of Meggido. The inevitable, as prophesied by Jeremiah, seemed destined to follow.

In the year 586 B.C. the city was besieged and burned by Nebuchadnezzar, and the inhabitants were carried away into Babylonian captivity. The prophet Jeremiah wept over its ruins and wrote his book which we call Lamentations.

For 50 years the city lay in desolation and ruins. Its only inhabitants were the wild beasts of the field, or an occasional wanderer who sought shelter among its ruins.

In 539 B.C. the Persians overcame Babylon, and three years later King Cyrus appointed Zerubbabel governor of Jerusalem and permitted him to return from Babylonia with about 50,000 Jewish exiles. These restored the altar and rebuilt much of their beloved city. Then in 520 B.C., under Haggai's and Zechariah's influence, the second temple (known in history as "Zerubbabel's Temple") was begun, and was completed and dedicated in 516 B.C. Seventy years later the walls were again repaired and rebuilt under Nehemiah in the incredible time of 52 days. The city then enjoyed peace for a prolonged period under the rule of the Persians.

Alexander the Great invaded Palestine in 332 B.C. and placed the Holy City under Greek influence; but after the death of the great general, his successors fought among themselves for it as a prize of war. In rapid succession Jerusalem fell to one weak ruler after another, climaxing with the wicked Antiochus IV Epiphanes (170 B.C.). He and his general, Apollonius, so desecrated the Temple and debased religion that in 165 B.C. the heroic Maccabeans captured the city. They destroyed its pagan altars, restored the Temple, relighted the perpetual lamp, and with ceremonies befitting the occasion rededicated it to God amid the rejoicing of the people.

Varying fortunes subsequently befell the city and the Jewish people for a full century while they were under their own beloved Maccabean rulers. In time two brothers, both laying claim to the high priesthood, quarreled and civil war broke out. Both brothers appealed to Rome for assistance against the other. Pompey, who was then at Damascus, marched on Jerusalem as a conqueror and, after siege which resulted in much destruction, took it for Rome in 63 B.C. In 54 B.C., Crassus plundered the Temple, but in 44 B.C. the walls were rebuilt.

In 37 B.C., Herod the Great was made ruler with Roman authority. Being a man of considerable ability, vision, and courage, he embellished many cities with magnificent public buildings, and to win the goodwill of the Jews he rebuilt Jerusalem and the Temple on the grandest scale ever to be undertaken. When complete, the Temple 19 appeared like a "mount of alabaster topped with golden spires." It possessed a bewildering range of porticos, grand gateways, double arches, and finely chiseled capitals, all of which covered 35 acres, and dazzled the eyes of all who beheld it. It was the pride of the Jewish people.

During the early part of the thirty-third year of Herod's reign, a Child was born in Bethlehem. Shepherds heard angels singing, "Glory to God in the highest, and on earth peace, good will toward men." Wise men came from the East to Jerusalem saying, "Where is he that is born King of the Jews? for we have seen his star in the east, and are come to worship him."[12]

That year, 4 B.C., according to the usually accepted chronology, Herod died and was buried four miles southeast of Bethlehem, on a beautiful hill called Herodium.

After growing to manhood, Jesus walked the streets of Jerusalem, prayed on the Mount of Olives, and taught in Herod's magnificent Temple, which He called "my Father's house." He taught of God, character, and destiny —rather than of marginal subjects such as art, science, and philosophy. He spoke as never man spoke, saying, "I am the way, the truth, and the life." Then He commanded His disciples to carry the good news to all men. One day He stood on the Mount of Olives and wept as He foretold the utter destruction of the city He loved so well.

Those of high authority in His own "church" brought about His arrest. Pontius Pilate presided over his mistrial, "washed his hands" before the multitude, and permitted the "Prince of Peace" to die on the lone, gray hill of Calvary just outside the walls of the city whose name meant "peace." The pitiful but immortal story of the tragedy of His crucifixion and the gladness of His resurrection forever ennoble the trend of human life. These events constitute the gravest and most momentous occasion in all the Holy City's history. Forever afterwards Jesus' birth and death stand at the crossroads of world history, and calendars are divided in such a way as to make His coming the central point of time.

From the Jerusalem school of the great Gamaliel, there arose one Saul, afterwards called Paul, who not only experienced true, divine regeneration of his inner self, but forged to the front as the greatest of theologians, and successfully led the Christian Church on the second stretch of its thrilling journey toward world evangelism.

In A.D. 41, Herod Agrippa, the grandson of Herod and Mariamne, was appointed king of Judea. Being a close friend of the emperor, and an idol of the Jews, he ruled for three years, with "unmixed popularity." His chief contribution to Jerusalem was the building of the "third wall," which began "at the Tower of Hippicus" (the present David's Tower), and went northwest to the Tower of Psephinus, then northeast "over against the monuments of Helena queen of Adiabene" (the present "Kings' Tombs"), and "the sepulchral caverns of the kings." The Romans suspected him of preparing for insurrection and ordered him to stop work on the wall. Shortly afterward, Agrippa suddenly passed away,[13] and, for the Jews, there followed one of the darkest periods in the entire history of Judea.

In the year A.D. 66, the Jews felt they could bear the odious burdens no longer. They threw off the Roman yoke and assumed nominal control of Jerusalem, along with many other cities of Palestine. The Roman legions under Titus, son of the Emperor Vespasian, besieged and captured city after city in the north, and in A.D. 70, shortly before the Passover, they surrounded Jerusalem and began one of the most terrible sieges ever recorded in the annals of men.

Titus commanded 54,000 legionnaires, along with thousands of Bedouin archers and Arab horsemen. The defenders mustered less than half this number of fighting men, and they were hopelessly divided into three factions, 21 each of which held a different section of the city, and periodically fought each other. The siege lasted for 134 days, while hunger, division, desertion, and death constantly menaced the overcrowded city.

Late in the summer Jerusalem fell, its sacred Temple was burned, and its people were slaughtered indiscriminately or led away as captives. The city was razed to the ground, and when Titus departed only the towers of Hippicus, Phasael, and Mariamne, and a portion of the wall were left standing to protect the Tenth Legion, which was left to guard the site. The rest of the city was dug up to its foundations.

For more than half a century Jerusalem lay desolate. Then, in 131, Emperor Hadrian ordered that the three towers left by Titus be destroyed and the city be rebuilt as a Roman town under the name of *Aelia Capitolina*. He would crush Jewish nationalism by obliterating Jewish Jerusalem forever. In indignation the Jews arose in rebellion under the leadership of Bar Cochba, "Son of a Star." The rebellion gained some ground, but was soon quelled in Jerusalem, and in the year 135 was finally put down in the bloody battle of Bethar *(Bettir)*, southwest of Jerusalem. After this the Jews resisted Rome no more.

When the rebellion was over, Hadrian and Tineius Rufus, the new governor of Judea, removed the towers of Hippicus, Phasael, and Marimne, ploughed up a portion of the Temple site, and, according to ancient Roman custom, laid out with a plough the outer boundary lines of the new city, and preceeded to make the site of Jerusalem into a heathen city. Old walls were rebuilt, new walls erected, and vast building operations were carried forth, of which the most objectionable was a temple to Jupiter, erected on the Temple site. In it were placed statues of Jupiter, Juno, and Minerva, and in front of the Temple was erected a statue of Hadrian on horseback. On the traditional site of Christ's burial, a vast terrace was constructed, and on this was erected a temple to the worship of Venus (Aphrodite). Within was a marble statue of the goddess. Outwardly the place was just another heathen city, and no more. Jews were forbidden to enter the territory under pain of death.

In A.D. 212, Bishop Alexander Flavian journeyed from his native Cappadocia and founded a Christian library in the city of Jerusalem (then called Aelia). A new form of piety arose—the desire to visit the holy places. Learned men like Origen and Julius Africanus came to Jerusalem and searched the whole of Palestine to "find the vestiges of Jesus, of his disciples and the prophets." Books were written of people and places. More pilgrims came, and the Church knew a few happy years before the beginning of the great persecutions of the third century.[14]

Under Constantine the Great (312-37), Christianity was established as the ruling religion of the Roman Empire, the name "Jerusalem" was restored, and the city given a worldwide importance that it has never lost. Helena, the mother of Emperor Constantine, came in person to Jerusalem, and under her care the Church of the Holy Sepulchre was erected, and Jerusalem became a Christian city to which waves of pilgrims came.

Julian the Apostate became emperor of Rome, and in A.D. 361 attempted to rebuild the Temple, but is said to have been prevented from so doing by an earthquake, or by a fire which burst forth from the subterranean passages within the foundation. This not only brought Julian's abortive efforts to an end, but the event was reported as a divine miracle, and greatly increased the flow of pilgrims to the city. More than ever it was regarded as being holy.

With the division of the Roman empire in 395, Jerusalem passed to the Greek empire, and for two centuries the city was the goal of Christian pilgrims who came from almost all lands where Christians were found. In A.D. 450, 23 the Empress Eudoxia, widow of Theodosius II, took up residence in Jerusalem and rebuilt the walls upon their ancient lines, including those around the Western Hill and the Pool of Siloam within the circuit. In 614 the Persians, under Chosroes II, captured Jerusalem, killed large numbers of monks and clergy, and destroyed the churches. Then Heraclius, the Byzantine emperor, took the field of battle, defeated the Persians, and rebuilt Jerusalem as a Christian city.

In 638, six years after Mohammed's death, the Arabs marched on Jerusalem, and it fell to them with little resistance. Journeying from Medina on a red camel, Caliph Omar, dressed like a son of the desert, joined his army encamped on the Mount of Olives, met Sophronius, the churchman who ruled Jerusalem, and granted him and the Christians the most humane terms ever given to Jerusalem by a conqueror. After eating a simple meal, Omar performed his devotions, then arose and entered the city of which the Arabs had long dreamed.

In memory of Mohammed's heavenly visit, the Mosque of Omar was ordered to be constructed over the site of the Old Jewish Temple, and Christians were given their churches and freedom of worship. Mr. Nuseibeh, a devout and reliable Moslem, was appointed keeper of the Church of the Holy Sepulchre, which has proven a pleasant arrangement, since descendants of that same Nuseibeh family have to this day exercised authority without partiality.

Six years later Omar was assassinated in Jerusalem, and in 688 to 691, Caliph Abdal-Melek replaced the Mosque of Omar with the beautiful structure known as The Dome of the Rock, which with care, repair, and remodeling has stood the ravages of time and war until the present.

In 969, Jerusalem fell to the Egyptians, and in 1077 it was captured by the Seljuk Turks. Their outrages stirred

Christendom, and aroused a religious enthusiasm in Palestine and Europe that culminated in the launching of the Crusades. In 1098 a Christian army, commanded by Godfrey de Bouillon, entered Syria in triumph, and in the following year laid siege to Jerusalem. The first attacks failed, and the Crusaders suffered from lack of water and provisions. At length the Genoese fleet reached Jaffa, and they supplied ample stores and men skilled in directing a siege. Within two weeks Jerusalem was captured, and a Latin kingdom established with Godfrey as king, although he refused to be crowned in the city where his Lord Christ had worn thorns. The Holy City then had peace which lasted for 88 years, under nine kings.

In time those who constituted the Christian kingdom of Palestine came to place large emphasis on outer trappings and relics such as "the true cross," and small emphasis on Christian experience and living. As a result, their power was diminished and Saladin, a merciful and mighty prince among the Arabs, defeated the Christian forces at Hattin near the Sea of Galilee, and marched on Jerusalem in 1187. After an eight-day siege the city fell to Saladin, who relieved the starving and permitted the inhabitants to evacuate in peace.

For 42 years the Arabs occupied Jerusalem; then Emperor Frederick II gained the city by treaty, and crowned himself king. Eleven years later it again passed to Mohammedan rule, and remained thus for three years, when it was again yielded to the Latins as a price for the promise of Christian aid in a contemplated war against Egypt. They rebuilt the walls, and extended them on the south to include the so-called Tomb of David. Only one year of peace had been enjoyed when, in 1244, the Khwarizmian hordes swept down from the north, took Jerusalem, massacred the people, and put an end to Christian occupation. The city soon reverted to the Arabs.

In 1517 the city was conquered by Selim I, sultan of

the Ottoman Empire, and remained in possession of the Turks for four centuries. In the last months of 1917, the British army under General Allenby encamped on Neby Samwil, four miles northwest of the city. Fighting of varied intensity took place west of the city, and on the Nablus road leading northward. On December 6 and 7 the fighting on the hills west of Jerusalem, and the rapid advance of a British force from Hebron, caused great excitement in the city. Toward evening December 8, the news that British troops had passed *Lifta* brought sudden panic in the ranks of the Turkish troops, who left the field of battle and hurried back to the city and down the Jericho road eastward. Joy filled the hearts of the Jewish people, and in some quarters the cry was heard, "The Turks are running; the day of deliverance is come."

Before dawn on Sunday, December 9, the Turkish governor hurried down the Jericho road, leaving behind him a letter of surrender. With this letter in his possession, and the white flag of truce (made of a bed sheet furnished by Mrs. Bertha Vester) fluttering over his head, the mayor of Jerusalem, accompanied by a few associates, set out westward. The group made contact with and surrendered to Sergeant Hercomb and Sergeant Sedgewick of the London regiment. They in turn took the mayor to General Allenby. As the sun arose, the mayor officially delivered the city to the British. The last Turkish soldier left Jerusalem at seven o'clock by the St. Stephen's Gate, and the Turkish power which had been supreme in the city for 400 years came to an end.

General Allenby, dressed in a simple khaki uniform, accompanied by his military staff and representatives from other Western nations, entered Jerusalem on foot the morning of December the eleventh by the way of the Jaffa Gate, and went immediately to the steps of the Tower of David and read a proclamation giving freedom of religious worship to all the peoples of the city, and assuring them of security while they went forward with their usual pursuits of life. Arab and Jewish joy knew no bounds.[15]

A military administration was instituted, and a Pro-Jerusalem Society organized. Everyone went forward with the task of repairing the walls and restoring to the city its erstwhile beauty and impressiveness. On July 1, 1920, Hon. Sir Herbert Samuel assumed office as the British high commissioner for Palestine, and a civil administration was established. The Council of the League of Nations approved the Mandate of Palestine on July 24, 1922, with Jerusalem as its capital. The city prospered, new homes were built, new industries established, and the population increased to almost 150,000 people of many nationalities and languages. The new city of the Jews grew up outside the walls to the west, and in time surpassed the old, both in size and in beauty of its buildings, but not for picturesqueness and impressiveness.

The United Nations Commission for Palestine, in 1947, recommended the partition of Palestine among the Arabs and the Jews. Jerusalem and its environs, along with Bethlehem, was to be set aside as an International Zone. The British decided to yield the Mandate, and shortly after sunrise on May 14, the Union Jack (Great Britian's flag) was hauled down from its staff over the Government House in Jerusalem. The British governor general, Sir Allen Gordan Cunningham, drove to the airport in his bullet-proof Daimler and flew to Haifa in an RAF plane, where he boarded the British light cruiser "Euryalus." Precisely at midnight, the ship passed the three-mile limit of Palestine's territorial waters. Thus after 31 years of noble and relatively unselfish work, the British left Jerusalem.

At exactly four o'clock, May 14, 1948, the Jewish National Council, under the leadership of Mr. David Ben-Gurion, met in the two-story Art Museum at Tel Aviv, where Ben-Gurion read their Declaration of Independence and proclaimed the establishment of the "Jewish State in Palestine, to be called Israel."

During the Arab-Jewish war which followed, the Arab Legions drove directly for Jerusalem and took over the Old City, which, to them, was next in importance to Mecca and Medina. The Jews held tenaciously to the New City, which by their efforts had grown up outside the walls, to the west and northwest.

When the armistice between the Jews and the Arabs had been signed, and the United Nations Trusteeship Council was preparing to establish the international regime over Jerusalem, the international planners were startled by the words of David Ben-Gurion: "There has always been and always will be one capital only—Jerusalem the Eternal. . . . Thus it was 3,000 years ago and thus it will be, we believe, until the end of time."

Abdullâ, colorful and cunning king of Jordan, declared: "The United Nations does not seem to know the reality of the situation. We oppose the internationalization resolution because it is impractical."

Thus it was, in December of 1948, that David Ben-Gurion bluntly defied the United Nations, and confidently moved the seat of his government and made New Jerusalem his capital. King Abdulla's Arab Legionnaires patrolled Jerusalem's Old City, which was made an intgral part of the Jordan Kingdom. The two governments pledged protection and access for all who would come from the ends of the earth to visit Jerusalem's historic sites which had been made sacred by selfless surrender to God's cause, and by the pilgrimages and tears of millions.

In August of 1949, the bones of Theodor Herzl, the prophet "Moses" of modern Israel, were brought from Vienna to Jerusalem and laid to rest in a sumptuous tomb on Mount Herzl, a high hill in the western suberbs of New Jerusalem.

In the six-day Arab-Jewish war of June, 1967, Israel's

JERUSALEM
IN NEW TESTAMENT TIMES

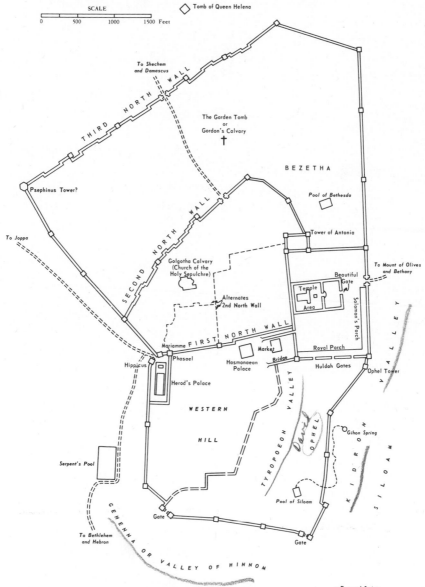

SCALE

Tomb of Queen Helena

0   500   1000   1500 Feet

THIRD   NORTH   WALL

To Shechem
and Damascus

The Garden Tomb
or
Gordon's Calvary

BEZETHA

Psephinus Tower?

Pool of Bethesda

SECOND   NORTH   WALL

To Joppa

Tower of Antonia

Golgotha Calvary
(Church of the
Holy Sepulchre)

To Mount of Olives
and Bethany

Beautiful
Gate

Temple
Area

Salomon's Porch

Alternates
2nd North Wall

Mariamne   FIRST   NORTH   WALL

Market

Royal Porch

Phasael

Hasmonaean
Palace

Bridge

Hippicus

Huldah Gates

Ophel Tower

Herod's Palace

WESTERN

KIDRON   VALLEY

HILL

TYROPOEON   VALLEY

David

OPHEL

Gihon Spring

Serpent's Pool

SILOAM

Pool of Siloam

Gate

GEHENNA   OR   VALLEY   OF   HINNOM

To Bethlehem
and Hebron

Gate

En-rogel Spring

armies moved so decisively that ancient Jerusalem was taken over in two days and a night. Finally, when the issues of war were certain, there rose the grand cry, "The Wall . . . the Wall!" And suddenly there came a crescendo of cheers. From that moment the major thought was centered on the Wailing Wall. Hundreds broke and ran down the narrow street, and stood weeping before the sacred Wall. The Israeli flag was raised over all the principal buildings of Jerusalem, except the Temple area with its Dome of the Rock and Mosque of Al-Aksa. This was left sacred to the Moslems. Ancient and modern Jerusalem and all their environs were declared a single city to be governed by Israel. The world gasped, as before its eyes was unfolding what could possibly culminate in the literal fulfillment of Christ's prophecy: "Jerusalem shall be trodden down of the Gentiles, until the times of the Gentiles be fulfilled."[16]

CHAPTER **2**

Famous Valleys of Jerusalem

The physical aspects of ancient Jerusalem and its environs may best be understood by thinking of the city as built on the southern termination of a *1,000-acre* Judean *plateau* or tableland, sloping slightly toward the southeast. This mountain plateau attains an average height of 2,500 feet above sea level, and is almost entirely cut off from the surrounding country by two gorge-like valleys that bear names familiar to us from 31 childhood—the *Valley of the Kedron* and the *Valley of Hinnom*—which encircle the city like two great arms thrown about it in protecting care. A third valley, not so long and not so deep, known as the *Valley of the Tyropoeon,* cuts directly through the city, cleaving it into two general parts, thus leaving the major portion of the city on two broad spurs of the plateau.[1]

Only on its north side was the city denied the privacy and security which deep, precipitous valleys afford ancient cities, but here Jerusalem had a many-towered wall and a moat attaining a depth of 50 feet, which served to deny the enemy ready access. These deep valleys, the moat, and the city's towering walls separating Jerusalem from the northern portion of the rocky plateau, of which it formed a part, gave strength to early Jerusalem and contributed to her subsequent greatness. These have ever been rare features in the general scenery about the Holy City. Out beyond these precipitous valleys is a rough triangle of higher mountain ridges which hide the city away in its mountain fastness. "As the mountains are round about Jerusalem, so the Lord is round about his people from henceforth even for ever."[2]

The *three* valleys and *five* hills within the city have much to do with fixing the bounds and determining the essential topography of Jerusalem. All else falls into line with these.

VALLEY OF THE KEDRON

This most interesting valley rises north of the city of Jerusalem in an insignificant depression known as *Wady el Joz,* or "Valley of the Walnuts." In its upper reaches it lies 2,600 feet above sea level, but soon takes a fairly graceful plunge eastward, then rapidly deepens while its precipitous sites are well-dotted with rock-hewn sepulchres. Here and there gaunt, twisted olive trees, rooted in the bare and stony ground, relieve the stern aspects of the landscape.

Pushing on eastward, the ravine reaches that section commonly known as the Valley of Jehoshaphat, where through the centuries enemy armies have often encamped against Jerusalem. After having flowed in an easterly direction for another one-half mile, the valley makes a circle and takes its course southward. Part of the way, as it passes in an irregular line parallel with the eastern wall of Jerusalem, it is smooth and broad and fairly well-covered with grainfields, threshing floors, and olive orchards. At one locality there are (or were) so many places for threshing grain that it is here sometime called The Valley of the Threshing Floors.

Just above the bridge, as the valley approaches the Garden of Gethsemane, it is so covered with trees and vines and flowers that the scenery would almost remind one of tropical verdure. While running parallel with the wall, and dividing Jerusalem from the Mount of Olives, the valley passes by the reputed tomb of Mary and the Garden of Gethsemane on its east side, and St. Stephen's Gate and the traditional place of the stoning of Stephen on its west. Here it is crossed by the road to Jericho, and from here on to its termination the valley, in ancient times, was known as the King's Dale.

Further on southward the Eastern Gate is passed, and the Kedron flows close to Mount Moriah and the Temple, from whence in ancient times came the odor of smoke, of incense, and of the burning sacrifices. On either side of the Brook Kedron are extensive, well-constructed, terraced slopes covered with grape vineyards, and fig and olive trees.

On the east, beginning far up on the slopes of the Mount of Olives and extending well down into the valley, lies the vast Jewish Cemetery with its many thousands of "whited sepulchres." Down beneath them all, nestling 33

Mount of Olives

closer to the brook, is the unforgettable monument known as Absalom's Pillar, which is in "the king's dale."[3] Then comes the Tomb of Jehoshaphat, the Grotto of St. James, and the Pyramid of Zachariah, and also the traditional tombs of Huldah, the prophetess, Haggai, and Malachi.

At the crest of the mountain is a peculiar, labyrinthine excavation called the "Tomb of the Prophets." Its principal cavity is a narrow, 150-foot-long, semicircular passage, on the outer side of which is a series of some 30 small tomb rooms. Many of the Jews regard these as of ancient origin, and revere them as the tombs of their prophets, yet the inscriptions are in Greek. Numerous generations of pious Jews, at least since the time of the first Temple, have craved to be buried in this the most famous of all Hebrew cemeteries. For 19 years (1948-67), the Jews were not permitted to be buried here, or to even visit the place. Now, since recapturing the ancient city, the Jewish people again have freedom of access to this, their cemetery, which to them is the most sacred of all burial places in the world.

At a point opposite the southeast corner of the old city wall, the valley becomes quite narrow and drops to a level of 2,300 feet above sea level, or 300 feet below its source. Its banks are steep, and the deepening valley displays a measure of wild, old-world beauty seldom seen in any but mountain uplands. The gray-green of fine olive groves, beautifully terraced vineyards, and stately, towering spruce cover the well-eroded hillsides once so steep and forbidding as to provide almost impregnable bulwarks against the siege of Jerusalem's great eastern and southern walls. Farther on the way, the stream bed has shifted about 80 feet eastward because of the debris that in ancient times was rolled or pushed into the valley. Also, the accumulation of rubbish during the ages has raised the surface level from 10 to 50 feet above the ancient bed to its present level.

35

Lower Kedron Valley with Garden of Gethsemane center, Mount of Olives rising behind, Jewish cemetery at right. Absalom's Pillar, Tomb of Jehoshaphat, Grotto of St. James (columns), and Pyramid of Zacharias at bottom. Jerusalem out of range at left.

Soon after leaving a point nearest the southeast corner of the city wall, and sweeping past the Temple mount, the valley swerves slightly to the west, then continues southward past the village of Siloam (on its left), and the ancient Gihon Spring, now called the Virgin's Fountain (on its right). From thence it goes through the King's Garden to the well En-rogel, or Job's Well, where it is joined at right angles by the Valley of Hinnom. Here the elevation is 2,000 feet above sea level. Thus the valley of the Kedron, less than two miles long, has fallen 600 feet from its source to the point where it joins the Valley of Hinnom, near En-rogel.

Valley of Hinnom

In ancient times this valley was often called "the valley of the son of Hinnom," and at other times it was called Tophet. At present it is known by the Arabs as *Wady er Rababi*, or Fiddle Valley.

The depression which makes up the Valley of Hinnom begins north of the city, a few hundred yards west of where the Kedron Valley takes it rise. At first the valley takes a southwesterly direction. Then, not far from the present post office building, it makes a circle through the Moslem cemetery. Here within the valley lies the pool known as *Birket Mamilla*, which is 290 feet long and 190 feet wide. The pool is partly hewn out of virgin rock and partly enclosed with walls of masonry. From it a hidden conduit leads southeastward to the Pool of Hezekiah in the heart of the Old City. The valley contains no springs and, therefore, is dry throught the year except in the rainy season— November to April. During the rains it is a catchment basin from which the water flows through the conduit to the old Pool of Hezekiah. Until recent years, the water in the pool was used for domestic purposes, but has now been condemned for sanitary reasons.

After leaving the Pool of Mamilla, the Valley of Hinnom is crossed by Mamilla Road; then it circles slightly southeastward until it nears Jaffa Gate, when it turns directly south. Leaving David's Tower on its east, and King David's Hotel on the west, the valley soon passes the southwest corner of the modern city wall. Here another pool is formed which is known as *Birket es Sultan*, or the Sultan's Pool. This pool is about 500 feet long, and is traditionally identified with the Lower Pool of Gihon, just as the Pool of Mamilla is spoken of as the Upper Pool of Gihon. Neither is correct, since *Gihon* means "gusher," and the Pools of "Upper" and "Lower" Gihon would in all probability have been located on the other side of the city, below Gihon Spring in the Kedron Valley. Here is found the only "gusher" or intermittent fountain in or near Jerusalem.

The old road to Bethlehem crosses the Valley of Hinnom just below the Sultan's Pool, and after this the valley deepens as it circles eastward and passes beneath the high bluff which forms a part of The Hill of Evil Counsel. A few hundred yards eastward, the valley passes The Field of Blood, which is located high up on an embankment to the right. A short distance farther on, Hinnom joins the Kedron and Tyropoeon valleys at the aforementioned well Enrogel, or Job's Well.

In Bible times, the Valley of Hinnom was used as a technical boundary line separating the tribe of Benjamin from that of Judah. "And the border went up by the valley of the son of Hinnom unto the south side of the Jebusite; the same is Jerusalem."[4]

The valley runs close by the west wall of the city, then circles about the southern side of Jerusalem, and therefore leaves the Holy City out of the bounds of Judah and well within the territory of Benjamin. The expression "Judah and Jerusalem," found in biblical records, is used because of the fact that Jerusalem did *not* lie in Judah. The Rabbinical tradition that the boundary line between Ben- 37 jamin and Judah ran through the heart of the city is un-supported by Old Testament evidence, as is well-known by most every Palestinian specialist and more careful students of the Bible. Only those portions of Jerusalem which had grown up outside the walls south and west of Hinnom could possibly have been considered a part of the Holy City. "O ye children of Benjamin . . . flee out of the midst of Jerusalem."[5]

Hinnom is a place of vast historical interest, albeit mostly gruesome in its aspects. Of all the scenes around Jerusalem there is none that conjures up so many tragic associations as this wild and rocky valley. Its cliffs, its rock-hewn sepulchres, and its gaunt, twisted trees are suggestive of its checkered past. First, it was known as a place where, in idolatrous rites, parents sacrificed children, especially the firstborn, to Moloch (II Chron. 28:3; 33:6; Jer. 7:31). This god, who was worshipped by the Moabites and Ammonites, was a fire deity of the Assyrians and Canaanites, and was described by Jewish tradition as being hollow and formed of brass; in appearance like a huge man whose "face was that of a calf, and his hands stretched forth." Milton describes it:

> Moloch, horrid king, besmeared in blood
> of human sacrifice, and parents' tears,
> Though for the noise of drums and timbrels loud
> Their children cries unheard, that passed
>   through fire
> To this grim idol—in the pleasant vale of
>   Hinnom, Tophet thence,
> And black Gehenna called, the type of Hell.

In his efforts to put an end to the abominations of Hinnom, King Josiah rendered the place ceremonially unclean by destroying the elaborately constructed altars and dumping on it human bones and other corruptions.[6] Other refuse of the city was then dumped here, and the furnace

38

fires were kept constantly burning to consume it. Intense was the heat employed both in the sacrifice of children and later in burning the refuse. Thus, nearby, at the southwest corner of the city wall, stood the Tower of the Furnaces.

The gruesome aspects of the valley and the everlasting burnings offered such a setting as to cause many Hebrew parents to point out Tophet to their children as a *likeness* or *type* of the eternal burnings that await the wicked who should miss the way of righteousness and be lost in the fires of hell.

At the height of his prophetic career, Jeremiah went into the valley, broke an earthen jar, and prophesied that the accursed place which had been "filled . . . with the blood of innocents" should no more be called Tophet, but the valley of slaughter, because so many of Jerusalem's inhabitants should be killed there. And his direst prophecies were fulfilled in the destruction of the city in 586 B.C. and in A.D. 70, when tens of thousands were butchered, or led away as captives.

South of the city, overhanging one of the deepest places in the Valley of Hinnom, is a great precipice beneath the Hill of Evil Counsel, where Judas is said to have hanged himself following the sale of his Master, A lone tree, standing on the desolate brow of the south precipice, is suggestive of the tragic hanging episode.

THE VALLEY OF THE TYROPOEON

This valley, so often mentioned by Josephus and other ancient writers, arose in an olive grove just a few yards outside of Damascus Gate. When well within the city, it deepened at a rapid rate, and ran southward on a line parallel with the inner or west Temple wall until it divided the city into two parts.

When David began his career in Jerusalem, this valley may have been the western and northwestern border

of the walled part of the city, and if so, it served as an all
but impassable moat. It was then considerably over 200
feet deep, when measured from the Western Hill, and
more than 120 feet deeper than the eastern hills of Moriah
and Ophel. In Solomon's day as well as Herod's, it divided
the Upper and the Lower City, and was spanned by broad
and beautiful bridges supported by immense arches. Remnants of two of these arches may yet be seen at the Western Wall of the Temple area. The one near the
southwestern corner of the Temple wall is known as
Robinson's Arch, and the other farther along the wall to
the north, as Wilson's Arch. One of the beautiful bridges
which once spanned the Tyropoeon Valley is thought by
some to have been Solomon's "ascent by which he went up
to the house of the Lord." The Queen of Sheba saw it and
was deeply impressed.[7] However, this is not at all certain,
for Solomon's palace was more likely located just south of
the Temple grounds.

Somewhere in the lower reaches of this valley, Herod
the Great built a kind of gymnasium, or place for athletic
games. This expressed his interest in Hellenistic culture,
but alienated the devout Jewish leaders. Deep down in the
valley, 20 to 80 feet below the present level, there ran an
ancient sanitary drainage system which the excavators
located during the last century. Higher up in the valley,
in ancient times, there seems to have been a "concealed
spring" whose water served many useful purposes.

This valley, which was once so deep and moat-like, is
now so nearly filled up with the accumulated wreckage
and rubbish of 40 centuries that it is but a shallow depression, scarcely discernible until it is well past the Dung
Gate. Here it deepens as it goes quickly down to the Pool
of Siloam, and on through the King's Gardens, where it
finally enters the Kedron just above where the Kedron and
the Hinnom valleys connect.

Beyond the well, the combined valleys of Kedron,

Hinnom, and Tyropoeon continue in a common gorge known as the *Wadi en Nar* (the Valley of Fire)—a burned ravine running steeply down through the barren Judean wilderness. It enters the Dead Sea just south of *Ain el-Feskhah* and ancient *Qumran,* where lived the Essenes of Dead Sea Scrolls fame.

CHAPTER 3

The Hills of the Holy City

Within the bounds of ancient Jerusalem there are *five* hills, each of which forms a most interesting section of the Holy City. To become acquainted with these hills and their historical and archaeological significance is to know much about those things which interest millions of Jews, Christians, and Mohammedans. These five hills are: *Ophel, Mount Moriah, The Western Hill, The Northwest Hill,* and *Bezetha.*

42

Ophel, the City of David

Ophel ("the hump") is the spur or eastern hill which runs due south and slightly to the west of the Temple area. It comprises about 13 to 15 acres and was the site of the original city of Canaanite Jerusalem which was built up here near the perennial spring of pure water called Gihon. In modern times it is called the Virgin's Fountain. Ophel was the home of the priest-king Melchisedec, who received tithes of Abraham on his return from the campaign in which he defeated "the kings of the east" and rescued his nephew Lot. It was also the stronghold of the Jebusites, from whom David took the city. On capturing the city, David "dwelt in the castle; therefore they called it the city of David." After this he "built the city round about, even from Millo round about: and Joab repaired the rest of the city."[1]

Jerusalem became the capital of the Hebrew nation and in those days was sometimes called Zion. Later David brought up the sacred ark of the covenant and placed it on the adjoining hill known as Moriah, which became the true or specific Zion, because it was the habitation of God's Shekinah presence. Evidently David's people made extensive use of the large Western Hill—just as Sargon, Sennacherib, and other kings made use of areas about their strongholds which were suitable for habitation, yet not so well fortified.

Here on Ophel, and perhaps on adjoining hills, David erected buildings, reared his family, and composed many of his immortal psalms. Here he prayed and sang his songs, and the inhabitants of Zion caught the sweet refrain as his royal fingers drew strains of harmony from his magnificent harp.[2]

Here also David walked one night on the roof of his palace and beheld beautiful Bathsheba on the roof of her residence on a lower level, and suffered his moral breakdown. Here came faithful Nathan saying to David, "Thou art the man." This pointed reproof, coupled with the work of an accusing conscience, brought David to repentance and restoration.

It was from his palace on Ophel that David fled during the insurrection led by his son Absalom. Also from this palace the watchman saw Adonijah, Joab, and Abiather go toward the well En-rogel, farther down the valley, to begin their abortive attempt to crown Adonijah as David's successor. From the selfsame palace the enfeebled king gave instructions for the crowning of Solomon, which was quickly consummated at the nearby spring Gihon.

King David died and "was buried in the city of David,"[3] supposedly on Ophel, not far from where "the steps go down" to the Pool of Siloam.[4] The location of David's sepulchre was known at least up until the time of Pentecost, for the Apostle Peter said, "His sepulchre is with us unto this day."[5] But it probably was lost sight of during the destruction of Jerusalem by Titus in A.D. 70, and that of Hadrian in 130-32. Thus David's sepulchre, along with the "tombs of the kings of Judah," has been so well-covered in the wreckage and rubble of the centuries that excavators have been unable thus far to locate any certain traces of them. Some think King David may well have been buried on the Western Hill, and that the reference to "the steps" were to those that "went down" to the pool from the Western Hill.

The hill Ophel is located almost entirely outside the modern wall, and in its present ruined state appears rather insignificant. And really it has always been small—too small a place for David and his army, and his people, and the many Jebusites which David permitted to continue there along with the Israelites. And Ophel is unthinkable as a place sufficient in size to accommodate *all* the people of Israel as they came up to Jerusalem each year to the feasts.[6]

44 The strong and imposing "City of David" (Ophel)

was, as many believe, only a part of the Jerusalem of David's time—albeit the most important part—just as the elevated and strongly fortified 25-acre "imposing palace area" of King Sargon II was only a part—but the most important part—of the 741-acre city of Khorsabad.[7]

In excavations here, Dr. Guthe distinguished seven kinds of masonry, which he assigned to different eras, from the most remote antiquity to the Byzantine period. During the past few years Dr. Kathleen Kenyon has been carrying forward more careful excavations at certain places on Ophel.

The Hill Ophel was the scene of a great engineering feat during the reign of King Hezekiah. The spring of Gihon, now know as the Virgin's Fountain, was the only living spring of any consequence in Jerusalem, but was outside the city wall. Knowing that Sennacherib was on his way to besiege Jerusalem, Hezekiah, having counseled with Isaiah, secured the assistance of engineers and workmen who tunneled an aqueduct from Gihon underneath the Hill Ophel to a lower level in the Tyropoeon Valley. The waters ran through this into the new-made pool of Siloam, which was inside the city walls. "Hezekiah also stopped the upper watercourse of Gihon, and brought it straight down to the west side of the city of David" "He made a pool, and a conduit, and brought water into the city."[8]

In 1880, while two boys played in the Pool of Siloam, they ventured up into the conduit a little farther than usual and saw, on the right wall of the tunnel, about 15 feet in from the Siloam entrance, an inscription cut into the stone which formed a part of the wall of the conduit. They reported their find to Dr. Scheck, and he and others took a "squeeze" of the six lines cut into the stone. When translated by Professor Sayce, they read:

> The boring through is completed. And this is the story
> of the boring through: while yet they plied the drill, each

Modern remnant of the Pool of Siloam with entrance to Hezekiah's Tunnel in the rear. Note steps coming down at right.

toward his fellow, and while yet there were three cubits to be bored through, there was heard the voice of one calling unto another, for there was a crevice in the rock on the right hand. And on the day of the boring through the stone-cutters struck, each to meet his fellow, drill upon drill; and the water flowed from the source to the pool for a thousand and two hundred cubits, and a hundred cubits was the height of the rock above the heads of the stone-cutters.[9]

This inscription is not only some of the oldest Hebrew writing known, but it is quite in harmony with the biblical account of the event.

About 265 years after the boring of Hezekiah's conduit, when Judah had returned from captivity, Nehemiah and his workers repaired the gates and steps down to the Pool of Siloam. Jesus, while passing through the Temple at Jerusalem, saw a blind man whom He sent to the Pool of Siloam to bathe his eyes and receive his sight.[10] A modern version of the pool is there today, at the foot of the Hill Ophel, in the valley of the Tyropoeon. When left undisturbed, its waters glisten in the sunshine as in the days of Hezekiah and as in the time of Jesus.

Dr. Bliss uncovered traces of the old biblical Pool of Siloam, and from these he estimated that it must have been about 70 by 70 feet. The present pool or reservoir is only 52 feet long by 19 feet wide. Here the women gather to wash their clothing and bathe their babies. Going farther into the conduit, they fill their pitchers and carry away water for the household supply. Bliss also found an ancient stairway of 34 stone steps leading up the west embankment to the Western Hill.

Just south of the Pool of Siloam is a large reservoir formed by building a dam across the valley. It is known as the Old Pool, and is connected with the upper basin by a rock-cut channel. Water from this reservoir is used for the irrigation of the King's Gardens in the valley below. Near the Old Pool is an aged, stone-propped mulberry tree, which marks the traditional spot where the prophet Isaiah was placed in a hollow log and sawn in two by the order of wicked King Manasseh. Few places in or about Jerusalem furnish so many interesting mementos of the past as the area of the Pool of Siloam.

MOUNT MORIAH, THE TEMPLE AREA

Mount Moriah is that conspicuous portion of Jerusalem which the Arabs call the *Haram esh-Sherif* (the Noble Sanctuary). It lies north of Ophel, opposite the Mount of Olives, and almost hangs over the valley of Kedron. In ancient times it comprised about 19 to 26 acres, but now there are 35 acres in the area. It is 2,425 feet above sea level. It is the focal point of interest for the Holy City, the most memorable spot on earth, and the only place honored of God through long ages as the "habitation of his holiness."

A tradition which first appeared in definite form in Josephus' writings, and is now almost universally accepted, says that this Mount Moriah is the same as "the land of Moriah" to which Abraham came in obedience and faith to offer his son Isaac. It was here that God rewarded him with the promise, "In thy seed shall all families [nations] of the earth be blessed, because thou hast obeyed my voice." It is generally believed to be the place where Melchizedek, king of Salem, officiated as "priest of the most high God," to whom Abraham paid tithes after the successful campaign to rescue his nephew Lot.

While they were yet in the wilderness, the Lord spoke to the people through His servant Moses, saying:

> But when ye go over Jordan, and dwell in the land which the Lord your God giveth you to inherit, and when he giveth you rest from all your enemies round about, so that ye dwell in safety;
> Then there shall be a place which the Lord your God shall choose to cause his name to dwell there; thither shall ye bring all that I command you; your burnt offerings, and

your sacrifices, your tithes, and the heave offering of your hand, and all your choice vows which ye vow unto the Lord . . .

Take heed to thyself that thou offer not thy burnt offerings in every place that thou seest:

But in the place which the Lord shall choose in one of thy tribes, there thou shalt offer thy burnt offerings, and there thou shalt do all that I command thee.[11]

The Hebrews had long been in the land before "rest" had been given them "from all their enemies round about." And when it did come, it was through David, who slew Goliath, took Jerusalem from the Jebusites, defeated or gained the goodwill of nearby nations, and brought unity and prosperity to Israel until there was rejoicing throughout the land. Ere long, while in the enjoyment of the good things which they had gained, Satan got David to shift his dependence from God to the numbers of soldiers and people at his command. A pestilence broke out as punishment of a broken command that they should not turn their attention to numbers, but to the Lord. At the height of the pestilence, Jerusalem was reached, and with the threatened ravages, the "Place" which God had chosen was revealed:

And when the angel stretched out his hand upon Jerusalem to destroy it, the Lord repented him of the evil, and said to the angel that destroyed the people, It is enough: stay now thine hand. And the angel of the Lord was by the threshingplace of Araunah the Jebusite.

And David spake unto the Lord when he saw the angel that smote the people, and said, Lo, I have sinned, and I have done wickedly, but these sheep, what have they done? let thine hand, I pray thee, be against me, and against my father's house.

And Gad came that day to David, and said unto him, Go up, rear an altar unto the Lord in the threshingfloor of Araunah the Jebusite.

And David, according to the saying of Gad, went up as the Lord commanded . . . [and] bought the threshingfloor and the oxen for fifty shekels of silver.

And David built there an altar unto the Lord, and offered burnt offerings and peace offerings. So the Lord was entreated for the land, and the plague was stayed from Israel.[12]

Later, in consideration for the entire "place," or land area about Moriah, David gave Araunah (or Ornan) "six hundred shekels of gold by weight."[13] Thus he secured for all time "The Place"—probably about 26 acres—which the Lord had designated through His angel and through Gad, the minister of David. "Then David said, This is the house of the Lord God, and this is the altar of the burnt offering for Israel."[14]

As the king's years advanced and the shadows of life lengthened, his energies were largely devoted to employing masons and carpenters, and all types of artisans needed to build the house of the Lord on Mount Moriah. Stones were cut in the quarries, iron was gathered in abundance, immense quantities of precious metals were contributed, and cedarwood was brought in great cargoes by the Sidonians. Then, under divine compulsion, David, the king, summoned all the princes of Israel and all the officers and the leading people to Jerusalem. He stood up before them and said:

Hear me, my brethren, and my people . . . I had in mine heart to build an house of rest for the ark of the covenant of the Lord, and for the footstool of our God, and had made ready for the building: but God said unto me, Thou shalt not build an house for my name, because thou hast been a man of war, and hast shed blood.

Howbeit the Lord God . . . hath chosen Solomon my son to sit upon the throne . . . and he shall build my house and my courts . . .

And thou, Solomon my son, know thou the God of thy father, and serve him with a perfect heart and with a willing mind: for the Lord searcheth all hearts, and understandeth all the imaginations of the thoughts: if thou seek him, he will be found of thee; but if thou forsake him, he will cast thee off for ever. Take heed now; for the Lord hath chosen thee to build an house for the sanctuary: be strong, and do it.

Then David gave to Solomon his son the pattern [plans] of the porch, and of the houses thereof, and of the treasuries thereof, and of the upper chambers thereof, and of the inner parlours thereof, and of the place of the mercy seat, and the pattern of all that he had . . .

All this, said David, the Lord made me understand in writing by his hand upon me, even all the works of this pattern. . . . Be strong and of good courage, and do it: fear not, nor be dismayed: for the Lord God . . . will be with thee; he will not fail thee, nor forsake thee, until thou hast finished all the work for the service of the house of the Lord. . . . there shall be with thee [the priests and the Levites, and] for all manner of workmanship every willing skilful man, for any manner of service: also the princes and all the people will be wholly at thy commandment.[15]

Turning back to the congregation, David, the king, said: "Solomon my son, whom alone God hath chosen, is yet young and tender , and the work is great: for the palace is not for man, but for the Lord God." Then, after pledging 3,000 talents of gold and 7,000 talents of refined silver from his own personal resources, the king made the appeal: "And who then is willing to consecrate his service this day unto the Lord?" The response was exceedingly gratifying.

Solomon's Temple

In the fourth year of his reign (approximately 966 B.C.), Solomon began to build the magnificent Temple, according to the plans and specifications given him by his father, David. Phoenicians augmented his forces with both men and materials. Especially helpful was Hiram, an Israelite, who's widowed mother had married a man of Tyre, a worker in brass. Under the leadership of this stepfather and other specialists in Phoenicia, he had developed God-given talents to become a famous artisan—one who was filled with wisdom and understanding, and cunning 51 "to work in gold, and in silver, in brass, in iron, in stone, and in timber, in purple, in blue, and in fine linen, and in crimson." He also learned to cooperate with the "cunning men" of Israel in the execution of the many useful and ornate things called for in the plans for the Temple as given by the Lord to David and passed on to Solomon.[16]

In order to gain space for the main structure of the Temple, Solomon laid vast walls of foundation stones around the 10-acre summit of Moriah. Then, pushing back to the lower levels of the 26-acre site, he built up great walls from the sides of the mountain, erected grand arches to support splendid courts and covered colonnades. Some vaulted foundation structures on the southeast were made into stables, and others toward the center made into great water reservoirs so vast that one was called "the sea." Some small ravines were filled with dirt, and pavements laid over all these until the entire area was made to conform more nearly with the higher portion. Only the 10 acres immediately about Mount Moriah's peak was brought to a 16-foot higher level. This was to be the immediate site of the Inner Temple itself. All the area other than this was brought to the lower level.

For seven and one-half years armies of workmen, superintended by the most skilled artisans of Phoenicia and of Israel, labored faithfully to build the magnificent structure according to divine plan. The massive stones were cut, polished, and fitted together at the quarries, and all the molds were made, and the objects of brass and gold were cast by Hiram in the Jordan Valley. All the work was done with such skill that the Temple was finished without the sound of "hammer nor axe nor any tool of iron" being heard on the precints so sacred to the millions who were to worship there.

When the Temple was completed and the Feast of Dedication announced, the people gathered from far and 52 near, filling all the Temple courts to standing room—only necessary passageways were left clear. Through these, and in an atmosphere of silent awe, came the elders of Israel and with them the priests who bore "the ark of the covenant of the Lord." Marching steadily on, they came to the Temple, and on through the holy place into the holy of holies, where they placed the ark in position—"even under the wings of the cherubims." [17] When the priests came out of the holy place, the singers, along with the musicians and trumpeters, lifted up their voices in praise to God, saying, "For he is good; for his mercy endureth for ever."

Then King Solomon stood on a specially prepared brass rostrum near the brazen altar, before the stately pyloned sanctuary. Then kneeling down, he spread forth his hands toward heaven and dedicated the Temple to God in one of the grandest consecration services ever to be conducted. This is "the house of God," the royal prayer so plainly and eloquently said—the central place where the people might bring to God their sacrifices, their sins, their selves, and their petitions in prayer. Even if they happened to be in some distant land, they were to confess their sins and look back to this place and pray. "And, please, God, would You hear these prayers and forgive and heal? Even the stranger who hears of Thee and fears Thee and calls to Thee; *that all people of the earth may know thy name, to fear thee.*"

"The glory of God filled the house." After this never-to-be-forgotten service was over, the people were permitted to see more of their Temple, and use its sacred precincts as prescribed by plan.

Could you have been privileged to be there, and to enter Solomon's completed Temple from the east, as it had always been necessary to do when entering the former Tabernacle, you would pass through the Eastern or Golden Gate. Here 950 years later, Jesus would pass on His triumphal entry. Entering the Temple area, you would find

Cross Section of Solomon's Temple

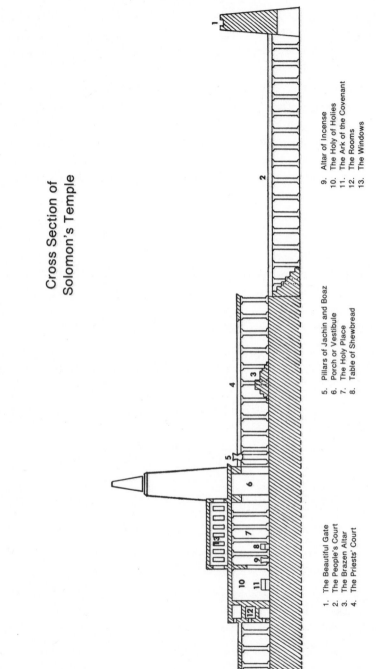

1. The Beautiful Gate
2. The People's Court
3. The Brazen Altar
4. The Priests' Court

5. Pillars of Jachin and Boaz
6. Porch or Vestibule
7. The Holy Place
8. Table of Shewbread

9. Altar of Incense
10. The Holy of Holies
11. The Ark of the Covenant
12. The Rooms
13. The Windows

yourself in the great Outer Court, or Court of the Gentiles, as it was commonly called. You would observe the spaciousness of the court, how it surrounded the entire Temple grounds, and was bordered by covered porches and colonnaded cloisters opening onto the inside of the court. The ceilings were richly carved, and at intervals there were other gates. Here, both in this spacious court and within the many "porches," persons of all nations were permitted to enter—even the money-changers, the sellers of doves, and other Temple merchants might enter anytime the Temple precincts were open.

Strolling a few paces along the courtyard, southward, then crossing the court in a westerly direction, you would come to a terrace on which the Inner Temple, the Temple proper, stood. Around its edge was a low stone wall, called the "Sarog" or "ritual fence." At intervals along the fence, there were steps leading to a higher level, but only those of the Hebrew faith might pass the fence line and climb those 14 steps. Signs here warned others not to go farther on pain of death. Two of those signs have been found in recent researches.

After attaining the higher level, beyond the steps, you would be faced with a lofty retaining wall enclosing the entire Inner Temple area, 280 feet long and 200 feet wide.[18] It had five gates and many towers, making it a fortified area of immense military strength, as well as a place of worship. Immediately before you would be its most important entrance—a richly ornamented double gate of dazzling bronze, with four polished pillars. In Solomon's day, writers praised its solidity and its beauty. In Jesus' day (in Herod's Temple) it was called the Gate of Nicanor, or simply the Beautiful Gate, which Josephus said it took 20 men to open each morning and close each evening.[19] It was here that Peter and John encountered the lame beggar, and Peter said, "Silver and gold have I none; but such as I have give I thee: In the name of Jesus Christ of Nazareth rise up and walk."[20]

The first court after passing through this gate into the Inner Temple, was the large Assembly Court, usually called the Women's Court, because the women could come only this far in the Temple. On three sides there were extensive overhead galleries or balconies arranged especially for the women so that they could see and hear most of what was said and done in the inner courts—especially when there was an assembly of worship with speaking in the court below. Here in Herod's later Temple, Jesus' mother brought Him for dedication; and here, during His public ministry, He often taught the people. Here the administrative affairs of the Temple were conducted, and on a lower floor nearby were the vaults where the Temple treasuries and Temple dues were kept. Also, near the pillars at the entrance were 13 treasury chests, into which Jesus "saw the rich men casting their gifts into the treasury . . . also a certain poor widow casting in thither two mites," and remarked that "this poor widow hath cast in more than they all."[21]

At the west side of this Assembly Court were 15 long, semicircular steps which led up into the Court of Israel, which was for men only. This narrow court (only 16 feet wide) led directly into the large sacred Court of the Priests, where were the great brazen altar of burnt offering and the brazen sea. The brazen altar was 15 feet high and 30 feet square, and stood, as is supposed, over the present Sacred Rock (under the Dome of the Rock). Here the animals to be offered for the sacrifices for sins were brought, and the priests offered them on this great bronze altar. The blood from these sacrifices ran down through a large, circular hole in the rock, into a small, rock-chiseled room below. (The circular opening in the rock and the rock-chiseled room remain today.) From a vent in the floor it is said there

ran a subterranean sewer, emptying the blood far down in

the Kidron Valley. At each of the four corners of this great altar was a horn, which symbolized mercy (I Kings 1:50; 2:28). Many within the adjoining courts could view the offerings being made, or at least see the smoke rising from the altar. Those who had brought the offering were always given a place of special advantage while their particular offering was being made.

The brazen sea was a great bronze bowl, seven and one-half feet high and 15 feet in diameter, with a capacity of some 10,000 gallons of water. It rested on the backs of 12 carved oxen, three facing each point of the compass. The water in the sea was for the special use of the priests, that they might cleanse the offerings and themselves before the offering of each sacrifice. All this took place in the Priests' Court, just in front of the sanctuary or Temple proper. It was here that the platform was built on which King Solomon stood during the dedication of the Temple.

The real Temple sanctuary, or building itself, stood on a terrace nine feet higher, with 10 steps leading up to its entrance. On either side of the steps were elaborately designed bronze pillars 37½ feet high and 12 feet in circumference. These two pillars were called Jachin and Boaz, indicating that Jehovah would give strength and stability.

The Temple itself was an imposing structure "of rare beauty and simplicity"—God himself having revealed the plans and specifications "in writing," and David passed them on to Solomon (I Chron. 28:11-12, 19). It was divided into three sections: the porch, the holy place, and the holy of holies.

The *porch* on the inside was a vestibule 15 by 30 feet, but on the outside it was the wide facade or front of one of the world's most momentous buildings. Josephus depicts Solomon as having made the foundation very wide, deep, and strong to support the grand facade. Both the Chronicler and Josephus picture Solomon as having built for the exterior of this porch a huge front, or pylon, of striking appearance, which towered some 180 feet above the foundation. Some modern scholars suppose these figures to be excessive, and at first thought the height would seem to present an architectural imbalance. Yet the pattern of the porch had received special attention when the plans were passed to Solomon.[22] And, too, special buildings before and since that time possessed imposing fronts. Herod built his Temple 150 feet high, then topped its front with a special 30-foot structure to help him attain the "altitude" of Solomon's Temple. Ammon's Temple at Thebes possessed a pylon, or front, 146 feet high; the Clock Tower in London's Parliament Building is 320 feet high; Old St. Paul's in London, with its lead-covered wooden spire, was 520 feet high; St. Peter's in Rome is 405 feet high (to the top of the cross, 448 feet); and the Washington Monument is 555 feet high. It should also be remembered that Solomon's Temple set the precedent for Christian churches, most all of which, until very recent times, had towering fronts, with very tall pinnacles or steeples.

The Holy Place. From the porch or vestibule, very wide doors of cypress wood, covered with gold, gave entrance to the holy place, which the Hebrews called the *hekhal.* The inside measurements of this sanctuary room were 60 feet long by 30 feet wide, and it was decorated with carved figures of cherubim, palm trees, and open flowers. In this holy place was the golden altar of incense. There was a gold horn on each corner where the priests burned incense morning and evening. The high priest placed a tip of blood on each horn once a year on the Day of Atonement. There was also the golden table of shewbread, on which were kept 12 loaves of fresh bread. On the opposite sides were the ten candlesticks of pure gold, five on the right side and five on the left. The incense symbolized morning and evening prayers rising to God; the horns represented the mercy of God ready to be shown in

58

forgiving man's sins; the shewbread stood for spiritual sustenance replenished each Sabbath; and the burning candles symbolized ample light along the righteous man's spiritual pathway.

The Most Holy Place. A beautiful veil or curtain of "blue, and purple, and crimson, and fine linen," with ascending angels painted on it, hung at the west end of the holy place. Beyond that mysterious veil was the most holy place—the holy of holies, or the oracle *(debir)*, as it was sometimes called. This room was a cube, 30 feet in each of its dimensions, and was ceiled with cedarwood, and all covered over with gold. Even the floor was overlaid with pure gold.

This was the innermost sanctuary, the most holy area within the Temple, and to all Israel the most sacred spot on the face of the earth. Jehovah had designated it as such.

Standing 15 feet high, with faces toward the veil, were two olivewood cherubim, glittering with overlaid gold. With outstretched wings, they stood at divine attention, so that a wing of each cherub touched the outer wall, while the other two wings met in the center of the room. Beneath the point where the two wings met, on a gold podium, sat the ark of the covenant, in which were the two stone tablets of the Law and the Covenant—God's words cut in stone—which Moses placed there. David had it in his heart "to build an house of rest for the ark of the covenant of the Lord, and for the footstool of our God," and here it rested. On the gold slab which served as a covering for the ark was "the place of the mercy seat," where God's Shekinah presence dwelt like a soft amber light emitting delicate opaline shadows and endless moving colors. Here God met man in mercy and atonement as the high priest came with blood, once each year, representing the people.[23]

Thus, court by court, and step by step, man was to come through the Temple approaching God. And this, the   59 focal point of the Temple, was the place of most importance—the place where one lone man, as representative of the people, met God once each year. What a sense of overwhelming awe the high priest must have had in this Presence! And what gravity attended his mission!

The two cherubim[24] who stood at divine attention in this most holy place were, along with the seraphim and the Ophannim, of the highest orders of angels in Hebrew angelology. They were angels especially endowed with power, wisdom, and prudence, who guarded the divine throne in heaven, flew missions of greatest gravity, and spoke words whose effect was next to God's words themselves (Isa. 1-7; Ps. 18:9; Gen. 3:24; Ezek. 1:6; Enoch 20: 7; 40; 61:10; 71:7).

What majestic ministers of the Most High were these representatives of all the angelic powers that constitute the "host of God," who in heaven guard the throne and sing His praises! Yet there they stood with stately bearing, guarding the most sacred spot on earth. Paul called them "the cherubim of glory" who stand overshadowing the mercy seat. Here was manifest the mystical Shekinah presence of the Holy and Almighty God in the midst of the city where He had chosen "to put his name there." All this was quite in harmony with the prophet Isaiah's later vision in this same Temple, where he "saw also the Lord sitting upon a throne, high and lifted up, and his train filled the temple. Above it stood the seraphims . . . And one cried unto another, and said, Holy, holy, holy, is the Lord of hosts."[25]

Angels had been in most all the important events of Israel, and were yet to be in many more. An angel had gone before them, in the wilderness, and had kept them in the way and had brought them to this place.[26] An angel with a drawn sword had stood on this very site and held David's attention while the prophet Gad had pointed it out to David as the appropriate place for sacrifices and the

Temple. How right and proper that now the likeness of *two* of the highest order of angels—cherubim—should stand in silent awe above the ark of the covenant and the mercy seat as symbols of the actual presence of God! An angel had appeared to Zacharias, while he ministered in the Temple, and announced the birth of John the Baptist. Angels would appear again at nearby Bethlehem to announce the birth of Christ, the Saviour, in whom man and God would meet. It was He who would "put away sin by the sacrifice of himself"—the true Offering and Atonement of which every sacrifice in the Temple was only a type. In confirmation of this, the beautiful and mysterious veil, separating the holy place from the holy of holies, was "rent in twain from the top to the bottom" the moment Christ yielded up his earthly life.[27]

Around the Temple sanctuary, on its two sides and at the back, Solomon built three stories of rooms, each seven and one-half feet high. Each of the three floors had about 30 rooms or vaults in which were kept the vessels and instruments employed in the sacrificial rites, and other objects not in regular use, as well as the gifts made to the Temple services. The main doorway on the south side, in the center of the building, provided a means of entrance and exit to these rooms, and a winding stairway provided means of ascent to the second and third floors.

If the general supposition is correct, south of the Temple, somewhere between the Temple and Ophel, Solomon built his Royal Palace and the Hall of Judgment. Here was the throne room where the king sat in judgment and where he personally received ambassadors and foreign guests. A gorgeous, subterranean passageway connected the king's palace with the Temple. This structural arrangement, among other things, deeply impressed the Queen of Sheba.

Around all the buildings, and all the courts on Mount Moriah, was a strong and imposing stone wall of great height, which was a part of the Temple complex. It made the entire area into a rather formidable citadel, sometimes called "the Temple platform."

For nearly four centuries this magnificent Temple stood, the pride and glory of the Hebrews, the admiration of surrounding nations, and the very habitation of God's holiness. The ark remained in its place during all this time, and no hand was laid on it, despite all the incursions made into the country by foreign militarists and royal gold seekers. Then, in 586 B.C., came Nebuzaradan, the general of King Nebuchadnezzar, with his great army of trained warriors. They destroyed Jerusalem. The stones of the beautiful Temple were rolled into the valleys below, the intricate carvings of woodwork burned, the gold and silver removed, and Moriah left covered with ruins.

No one knows what became of the ark. Some supposed it was hidden in some subterranean cavern beneath the Temple, but if so, no survivors seem to know where. The writer of Second Maccabees suggests that the prophet Jeremiah removed it beforehand, in the hope that it might be concealed in some safe place. A cave in Mount Nebo was suggested as the probable hiding place, yet no remains of it have been found.[28]

Zerubbabel's Temple

On returning from the Babylonian exile in 536 B.C., the Hebrews wept when they saw on Mount Moriah the ruins of their former Temple. In the seventh month after their return, they devoutly erected an altar, and during the beginning of the second year they laid the foundation stones for a second Temple, but were stopped because of opposition by the Samaritans. They did little more about the matter, however, until 520 B.C., when, under the prodding influence of the prophets Haggai and Zechariah, and with funds furnished them by King Darius I of Persia, they carried forward the construction of the *second* Temple, which was completed and dedicated in 516 B.C. It was an impressive building—strikingly similar in many respects to the first Temple. Yet the older men wept when they saw how poor it was in comparison with Solomon's Temple. It was called Zerubbabel's Temple, and served well as "the house of God," and as a rallying point for the Jews for almost 500 years. It was this Temple which the wicked Antiochus Epiphanes seized in 170 B.C. and desecrated with pagan altars. However, the God-fearing Jews rallied under Maccabean leadership, recaptured and cleansed the Temple, relighted the perpetual lamp, and rededicated it all to God.

Herod's Temple

Herod the Great—half Jew and half Edomite—was cruel and unscrupulous; yet he was capable, energetic, and ambitious—a man of great action. After having built or rebuilt Samaria, Masada, Machaerus, Ascalon, Caesarea, and his own gorgeous palace at Jerusalem, he assembled the leaders of the Jewish people and advised them that he had in mind to build them a new Temple.

Some of the leaders were very uneasy about his intentions, lest he remove their Temple, old though it was, and leave them without a central place for worship and sacrifice. To counter this, Herod very tactfully pointed out that:

> Our fathers, indeed, when they had returned from Babylon, built this temple to God Almighty, yet does it want sixty cubits of its largeness in altitude; for so much did that first temple which Solomon built exceed this temple: nor let any one condemn our fathers for their negligence or want of pity herein, for it was not their fault that the temple was no higher; for Cyrus, and Darius, determined the measures for its rebuilding; they [our fathers] had not the opportunity to follow the original model of this sacred edifice, nor could raise it to its ancient altitude; but since I am now, by God's will, your governor, and I have had peace a long time, and

have gained great riches and large revenues, and, what is the principal thing of all, I am at amity with, and well regarded by, the Romans . . . I will do my endeavours to correct that imperfection . . . and to make a thankful return, after the most pious manner, to God, for what blessings I have received from him, by giving me this kingdom, and that by rendering his temple as complete as I am able.[29]

To further remove their fears, he assured them that he would respect the traditions and sanctity of the place, would train 1,000 priests as stonecutters, carpenters, metalworkers, and decorators for the work on the inner sanctuary and the holy of holies. Furthermore, he would not pull down any part of the Temple until all the materials were prepared and on hand for the reconstruction. Then he would take down only one section at a time and rebuild it before another section was touched, so they would enjoy an unbroken continuity in Temple worship and in the sacrifices. With these pledges, they consented, yet inwardly many would warily watch.

In the eighteenth year of his reign (20 B.C.), Herod began the training of 1,000 priests, employed 10,000 skilled masons, and had 1,000 wagons hired to haul the stone from the quarries where it was cut and dressed. He constructed piers and pylons and arches, and extended the broad walls 90 to 125 feet deep, about the steep southeastern, southwestern, and northeastern corners of the Temple area. He arched over and made stables of the deep cavities at the southeastern portion and formed large lower rooms at the southwest. The northeast corner was dirt-filled. Leveling and paving went forward on the area until it was brought to its present size of 35 acres.

To give protection to the Temple area, and to provide security for the treasuries and valuable vestments of the Temple, Herod built the Fortress or Castle of Antonia —named in honor of Mark Anthony—at the northwestern corner of the Temple Mount on the site of the ancient

Fortress Baris. Roman soldiers were stationed here and

steps gave ready access to the outer court. An underground passage led into the Inner Temple courts.

After reconstructing and enlarging the 10-acre Temple platform, laying out the Great Court, and enclosing the inner courts with marbled balustrades and walls, Herod took the 1,000 trained priests and began work on the main Temple sanctuary.

As each section was torn down and the debris removed, the new began to replace the old. It was a task of gigantic proportions, and a most delicate and unusual undertaking, yet Herod remained true to his pledged word. With the help of the priests, he rebuilt the Inner Temple in strict observance of the Solomonic tradition as to plan and ritual. The facade or front of the "porch," or vestibule, was constructed of marble adorned with gold, and towered 150 feet high. Above this, one or more "pinnacles" seem to have extended upward for about 30 feet until they matched the "altitude" of Solomon's Temple.[30]

The inside measurements of the porch, the holy place, and the holy of holies were the same as those of Solomon's Temple; only the outside was larger. The inner and outer courts were doubled in size, and enhanced in appearance. The holy place had its seven-branched candlestick (candelabra), the table of shewbread, and its altar of incense; but the holy of holies had no furnishings other than the beautful "blue, and purple, and crimson" veil at the entrance. At the place where the ark with the mercy seat had stood was a large, stone slab (some say a gold slab) on which the high priest sprinkled blood once each year on the Day of Atonement. The long-lost ark of the covenant was not available, of course; and there was no need of the cherubim without the ark and the mercy seat.

The Temple proper was completed and dedicated in 18 months. But it took about 45 more years to finish the elaborate work on the subsidiary buildings, the enlarged courts, the marbled colonnades, the cloisters, the "porches" (such as Solomon's Porch on the east, and the Royal Porch on the south), and the eight gates that pierced the mammoth, yet beautiful walls which enclosed the entire 35-acre plot.[31] In size and magnificence it exceeded Solomon's Temple.

What an impressive sight the Temple complex on Mount Moriah must have presented! And to climax all of its grandeur, in the center of the Inner Temple courts—at the very highest portion of the Mount—there stood the main Temple sanctuary with its 150-foot-high porch, and probably its 30-foot higher pinnacles. This imposing facade of marble and gold was so gleaming that it appeared from afar as a "mountain of snow glittering in the sun." It was the pride of the Jewish people, and one of the most magnificent temples ever known. Josephus says that in his day it was a common saying that a person had not seen anything until he had seen Herod's Temple.

It was to this Temple that Jesus was brought by His mother for dedication when He was but a child 41 days old; and here, when a lad of 12, He sat "in the midst of the doctors, both hearing them, and asking them questions."[32] It was here that Satan, wicked and politically minded as he was, brought Jesus from the wilderness of temptation, "up into the holy city," at the beginning of his ministry, and set him "on a pinnacle" of this very Temple, and said unto him: "If thou be the Son of God, cast thyself down: for it is written, He shall give his angels charge concerning thee: and in their hands they shall bear thee up, lest at any time thou dash thy foot against a stone."[33]

What a mundane spectacle! How impressive it would have been, from a human point of view, for the Messiah, at the very beginning of His public career, to have leaped unhurt from a position so lofty and so sacred—and that before the eyes of the thousands of worshippers and visitors at the Temple! But how foreign to Jesus' person, purpose, and mission!

His triumphal entry through the Eastern Gate led into this Temple, and from it He drove the merchants and money changers. Here he often taught the people, and in it He felt sufficiently at home to call it "my Father's house." One day, after completing His teaching in the Temple, He was leaving when His disciples said unto Him, "Master, see what manner of stones and what buildings are here!" Jesus answered saying: "Seest thou these great buildings? there shall not be left one stone upon another, that shall not be thrown down."[34]

His prophecy was fulfilled, when in A.D. 70, shortly before the Passover, Titus and the Roman legions surrounded the city, placed battering rams against the walls, and by late summer beat the city into submission. The beautiful Temple was burned and its people slaughtered indiscriminately. The city was razed to the ground, and when Titus departed, only Herod's towers—Hippicus, Phasael, and Meriamne—and a portion of the wall were left standing. In A.D. 135 the Emperor Hadrian removed the three remaining towers, cleared the city of rubbish, and erected a temple to Jupiter on Mount Moriah, but it stood only a relatively short time.

Julian the Apostate, youngest son of Constantine the Great, attempted to rebuild the Temple on Mount Moriah, that the prophecy of Christ might be falsified, but his efforts were said to have been frustrated by fire bursting forth from the numerous subterranean passages, driving away the workmen and compelling them to abandon their work.

The Dome of the Rock

When Caliph Omar entered Jerusalem in A.D. 638, he ordered the rubbish and filth cleared from the Temple site, and a mosque erected over the "Sacred Rock." The place was especially significant and sacred to the Mohammedans, because it was where Abraham went to offer Isaac 67 and where Ornan the Jebusite had a threshing floor on which David erected an altar at the time of pestilence. It was also where the three Temples had stood, and where (according to Moslem legend) the prophet Mohammed had prayed, and from whence he had ascended to heaven.

This building remained until 688, when Caliph Abdel-Malek removed the old wooden structure known as the Mosque of Omar. After collecting large sums of money, he began the erection of a magnificent building which he completed in 691 and named the Dome of the Rock. It was an octagonal structure with a 65-foot-wide dome overlaid with gold, and supported by many pillars and columns. The decoration of both its interior and exterior were masterpieces of Moslem art. Hundreds of workmen—Moslems, Jews, and Christians—were employed to care for the building and its carpets. These workmen were exempt from payment of taxes.

In the year 1016, an earthquake shock caused the Dome to collapse, but it was rebuilt six years later by Caliph Hakem.

When the Crusaders captured Jerusalem in 1099, they turned the Dome of the Rock into a Christian church, and called it the Temple of the Lord. It served as a model for many churches which were later erected at various places in Europe.

In the year 1187, Saladin captured Jerusalem from the Christians and, after having every vestige of Christian occupation removed (except the iron grill around the Sacred Rock), he put the building back to its former use as a place of Moslem worship. He covered many of the walls with marble, restored and embellished the building in general. Chief additions were the fine mosaics on the drum of the dome and the beautiful pulpit adjoining the prayer niche. The Haram area has remained in Moslem hands ever since, for although Jerusalem was again occupied by Christians, this time by the Crusaders in 1229-44, their occupation never extended to the Temple area. Or, if so, then not for long.

The Mamelukes, in the fourteenth and fifteenth centuries, covered the doors with copper, and repaired the dome, which caught fire in 1448 and collapsed, even though "all Jerusalem rushed to save it."

During the illustrious reign of Suleiman the Magnificent (1520-66), he carried out a wholesale renovation of the Dome of the Rock, added many beautiful windows, and decorated the exterior of the shrine with thousands of the most beautiful blue Persian tiles ever produced

Dome of the Rock, magnificent Mohammedan mosque built upon the site of Solomon's and Herod's temples at the summit of Mount Moriah.

in Oriental lands. Since then, the building has undergone different restorations, which have, for the most part, marred rather than enhanced its beauty. Just recently, however, the building has undergone the most extensive and far-reaching renewing and remodeling of its entire existence. It now stands in its beauty and sacred impressiveness as one of the world's finest and most delicately fashioned buildings, and "next after Mecca the most sacred building in Moslem lands."

It stands in the center of an irregular five-acre, stone-paved platform whose level is about 12 feet above that of the surrounding Temple area. Around it stand numerous small edifices—fountains, prayer niches, pulpits, and minor shrines. The platform is approached from each of its four sides by a flight of broad steps surmounted at the landings by graceful arcades, known as *Mawazin* or "scales." This is based on the Moslem belief that on the Day of Judgment the scales, with which God will balance the good and evil in men's lives, will be suspended there.

This Dome of the Rock, often erroneously called the Mosque of Omar, is an octagonal building, each side of which measures 66 feet. It is 528 feet in circumference, and 176 feet in diameter. The symmetrically designed, gold-plated dome crowning the building reaches 108 feet from the ground, and is surmounted by an artistically designed crescent 12 feet high.

The walls of the building are 36 feet high, the lower 16 feet of which are cased in marble, and the upper portion adorned with blue-, red-, and gold-colored tile so arranged as to form a harmonious design. Each of the eight walls forming the octagon are ornamented with seven round arches, 38 of which are pierced with windows, and the remaining 18 are blind panels.

This grand edifice has four entrances, each of which faces one of the points of the compass: on the west, the
Bab el Gharb (West Gate); on the north, the *Bab el Janna*

The "sacred rock"—the summit of Mount Moriah—directly under the Dome of the Rock. This is where Abraham prepared Isaac for sacrifice and where David built his altar.

(Gate of Paradise); on the east, the *Bab Daud* (Gate of David); and on the south, the *Bab el Qibla* (South Gate).

In the center of Mount Moriah, directly under the great Dome, lies the bare rock in all its massiveness—a huge ledge of rough, gray limestone 57 feet long and 43 feet wide, known to millions as the Sacred Rock. This is 71 unquestionably the summit or central peak of Mount Moriah, where once stood the Temples of Solomon, Zerubbabel, and Herod. What a rock! And how significant as *the* place where sacrifice for sin was made before the coming of Christ, the Lamb of God.

A great, round hole chiseled through this great stone (see photo) is shown as the place where the blood and refuse of the daily sacrifices flowed down into a room underneath. Under an archway nearby, at the southeast side of the rock, is a flight of 11 steps which lead down to this rock-hewn room where the blood collected, then flowed through a vent chiseled in the lowest place of the floor, and ran away to the nearby sewer in the Valley of the Tyropoeon, or as some say, into the Valley of Kedron.

The Great Mosque of El Aksa

This mosque is directly south of the raised Temple platform and is built against the southern wall of the Temple area. The original structure was a Christian church, built in the form of a cross by Emperor Justinian in the fourth century, and called St. Mary's Church. Then, after the Moslems took over in A.D. 638, they felt the need of a suitable building for common prayer and preaching. Neither the earlier building known as the Mosque of Omar nor the later and more stately Dome of the Rock fulfilled these needs. Therefore, sometime around 700, Caliph Al Waleed rebuilt St. Mary's Church, which was then in a somewhat ruinous state, and enlarged it to 272 by 184 feet. In the process, the form of the cross was obscured and it became a long, hall-like structure with 280 fine marble columns and many beautiful arches. It contains a vast amount of fine mosaic work, and has a beautiful silver dome. The building was shaken by an earthquake and rebuilt during the eighth century, reconstructed in 1034 by Caliph Al-Zahir, and greatly altered during the time of the Crusades. It was restored by Saladin, and partly

Solomon's Stables under the southeast corner of the Temple area. There are 88 columns in 12 rows. Originally built by Solomon or Herod and reconstructed in their present form by the Crusaders.

rebuilt in recent times. Its interior furnishings attract many, especially its brilliantly decorated dome and its minbar (pulpit) which was carved in Damascus, consecrated in Aleppo by Nur-ed-Din, and brought here by Saladin when he restored the Mosque. The Mosque of El Aksa has the form of a basilica of seven aisles, and accommodates about 5,000 worshippers. To the Moslems it is the most highly venerated mosque after the Kaba in Mecca.

Directly beneath the main Temple site are many underground caverns—some extensive and very well finished. The Jewish rabbis have a tradition that the original copy of the Law is buried within one of these sacred enclosures. It is also commonly believed that the ark of the covenant, which disappeared when Nebuchadnezzar's armies destroyed Solomon's Temple in 586 B.C., was concealed by Jeremiah and still lies hidden in one of these caverns beneath the Temple.

Underneath the southeast portion of the Temple area are the vaulted structures known as Solomon's Stables. These are made up of 100 ancient stone piers, about 28 feet high, and vaulted over with stone arches. They form 12 parallel rows of aisles or "stables," each row being 200 feet long. The entire width of the structural complex is 273 feet, from east to west. Most of the stones are of the Herodian pattern. The evident purpose of their original construction was the elevation and enlargement of the Temple area, but in the Middle Ages these were used as the stables of the French kings and of the Templars. The rings to which they attached their horses still exist. Herod probably stabled his horses here, and the tradition could be true that Solomon used them (or similar ones on a lower level) as stalls for the many horses which were "with the king at Jerusalem." At least the Horse Gate was in the nearby wall during the life of Solomon's Temple.

The Temple area possessed a splendid water system with cisterns and reservoirs which literally honeycombed the underlying area between the Dome of the Rock and the Mosque of El Aksa. Warren and Wilson measured and charted 30 of these. One reservoir of this system, known as the Great Sea, has an estimated capacity of 2 million gallons. Most of the water supplying this system came in conduits from the Pools of Solomon nine miles south of

The Western Hill of Jerusalem with the Tower of David in the foreground. The Temple Mount is in center and Mount of Olives beyond.

Jerusalem. These pools are continually fed by clear, sparkling water from the Sealed Fountain. The records indicate that Herod, the Crusaders, the Turks, and the British government repaired or reconditioned this aqueduct in order than an adequate supply of water might always be available here in the Temple area. For those who were permitted to come in, the water was also available for use in the nearby homes of Jerusalem.

THE WESTERN HILL, OR UPPER JERUSALEM

The Western Hill, which in ancient times was known as the Upper City, and in modern times as Mount Zion, is the finest of the two promontories extending upward from the main plateaus on which the city of Jerusalem is located. It is just across the Tyropoeon Valley, westward from Ophel and west and southwest from Mount Moriah. It covers nearly 100 acres, where Ophel covers only about 13 acres. It is 120 feet higher than the Temple area of Moriah, about 200 feet above Ophel, and is broader, more stately, and has far more open spaces than the crowded quarters of the Lower City.

The records do not clearly state just how the Western Hill was occupied during the time of the Jebusites, nor are they clear as to its occupation during the reigns of David and Solomon. They do indicate, however, that the Valley of Hinnom was the south and the west border line of the city of Jerusalem, which would indicate that the Western Hill was an integral part of Jerusalem. "And the border went up by the valley of the son of Hinnom unto the south side of the Jebusite; the same is Jerusalem: and the border went up to the top of the mountain that lieth before the valley of Hinnom westward, which is at the end of the valley of the giants northward" (Josh. 15:8).

Also, in speaking of the ancient city, Josephus says:

The City of Jerusalem was . . . built upon two hills which

are opposite to one another, and have a valley to divide them asunder; at which valley the corresponding rows of houses on both hills end. Of these hills, that which contains the upper city is much higher, and in length more direct. Accordingly, it was called the "Citadel" by King David; he was the father of that Solomon who built the Temple at first.[35]

Some are strongly inclined to believe that these statements were given in order to confirm that the Western Hill was a part of Jerusalem. Although perhaps sparsely settled in the time of the Jebusites, it was thickly populated during David's time. In fact, without this Western Hill there would not have been sufficient space to accommodate David and his army and the people who lived in Jerusalem, let alone those who came at the time of the feasts. The city's name in Hebrew—*Yerusalayim*—has the dual ending, which some think could conceivably refer to the "upper and the lower city" so often referred to in history.

When Solomon came to the throne, he married the daughter of Pharaoh, constructed his royal palace, and built "the house of the Lord" on Moriah, and then built "the wall of Jerusalem round about," and "repaired the breaches of the city of David his father" (I Kings 3:1; 9:15; 11:27). Some believe that he built some fine bridges which spanned the Tyropoeon Valley and connected his magnificent palace and courts and the sacred Temple precincts on Mount Moriah with this Western Hill. But no certain traces of his works on the Western Hill have been located.

Here, on this Western Hill, near the site of the ancient Corner Gate (the present Jaffa Gate), Herod the Great constructed his new palace, and along with it the famous fortified towers of Hippicus, Phasaelus, and Meriamne previously referred to. Here also—probably within this palace of Herod—was the Praetorium or residence and judgment hall of Pilate, the later provincial governor. Ordinarily the governor lived and held court at his palace; 77

therefore, it could well be that the soldiers took Jesus here for trial before Pilate. At least one tradition describes Pilate as holding his tribunal in Herod's Palace, and many scholars regard it as the place of Jesus' trial.

The palaces of the Hasmoneans and those of Agrippa and Bernice were eastward from the governor's palace. Southeastward along the hill was the palace of the high priest, Caiaphas, and not far away was the home of Mary, her husband ("the good man of the house"), and their son, Mark. In this home was the large guest room which was used by Christ and His apostles for their last Passover supper together. This same "large upper room"—if tradition may be trusted—was where the disciples were assembled "when the day of Pentecost was fully come," and where the young Church continued its worship services during the days of the apostles. Tradition reaching back to the second century says that later a church was built on the site. This was destroyed and restored a number of times, and in its present form was reconstructed by the Franciscans in 1333, and taken over by the Mohammedans in 1547.

Underneath the chapel is a rather imposing tomb or cenotaph which is known as the Tomb of David. The presumed location of the Upper Room carries a rather high measure of probability as to its authenticity, and the Tomb of David less. Yet both traditions are believed in sincerely, and have become exceedingly sacred to millions of Jews, Christians, and Mohammedans.

On his way from the Last Supper room to Gethsemane, Jesus would have crossed a part of this upper city where a portion of what was once a fairly prominent street has recently been discovered. This has been laid bare by the Fathers of the Assumption, and is now shown as an actual street through which Jesus may well have passed.

Toward the end of the fourth century A.D., a basilica called Holy Zion, Mother of all Churches, was constructed on a site adjoining the supposed Upper Room building. Pilgrims venerated the church and thronged it with the supposition that it stood on Mount Zion. Thus a tradition soon became current, and has long persisted, that the Western Hill was Mount Zion.

The Medeba Map, a sixth-century pictorial map of the Holy Land, with a special panel for Jerusalem, not only shows this splendid Western Hill well-covered with fine churches and other buildings, but shows it to be the main part of the city. One great church of that time was situated on one of the highest points. It had enormous foundations and took 12 years to construct. On November 20, 543, it was dedicated to St. Mary, mother of God, and long remained as one of the principal landmarks of the city. Yet nothing remains of it today. In fact, it is now impossible to determine the exact location of this fine basilica. If so many of these fine buildings built from A.D. 550 to 600 cannot be even traced today, then no one can say with certainty that buildings did not exist there in the time of King Solomon or in the time of David, or even in Jebusite times.

Much of this long, broad hill lies outside the present walls, yet the foundations and lower portions of ancient walls encircling the entire Hill have not only been traced, but excavated. In recent decades the Hill has been explored by archeologists in a small way in various places, but so many new buildings are now springing up on most of the vacant areas that thorough investigations are becoming all but impossible.

THE NORTHWEST HILL, OR AKRA

Just north of the Western Hill runs the western arm of the Tyropoeon Valley, which begins near the Jaffa Gate and, following the line of the present David Street, connects up with the Tyropoeon Valley near the north end of the Wailing Wall. Lying north of this deep, broad fork

Looking across the Northwest Hill section. Dome of the Church of the Holy Sepulchre is in lower center, new Arab city in background, and Mount Scopus in distance.

of the valley is the Northwest Hill, which projects down from the northwest like a promontory. Here stood the "Akra of the Syrians," which fell to the Maccabees in 142 B.C. The highest point in this area is not more than 2,480 feet above sea level, which is considerably lower than the Upper City.

In excavations carried on here between 1934 and 1948, towers and walls were found underlying ruins of the Herodian-style masonry. The excavators considered it reasonably certain that these walls and towers were those of the long-looked-for Hasmonean palace.

However, very little excavational research has been done in this area to ascertain what ancient ruins may or may not be found, the reason being that it is the Christian quarter, and is quite crowded with modern buildings— churches, convents, church offices, and many other buildings, both sacred and secular. But the one building site here that tingles with worldwide interest is that of the Church of the Holy Sepulchre.[36]

The Church of the Holy Sepulchre

In A.D. 312, Constantine was supposed to have had a vision of a cross in the sky, on which were the words, "By this conquer." He made the cross the standard of his army, after which such phenomenal success attended his efforts that in time he became the master and monarch of Europe and western Asia. Desiring to pay his debt to Christ and Christianity, he sent his mother, Helena, to the Holy Land in 326 to search for the tomb in which Christ had been buried. With the aid of Eusebius, bishop of Caesarea, and Macarius, bishop of Jerusalem, the debris was removed from a mound where had stood a temple erected by Hadrian to Aphrodite, the goddess of love. Here they are said to have found "three crosses," and other "evidences" which led them to designate the place as Calvary. Nearby they uncovered a tomb which they felt certain was the one in which Christ had lain.

Helena and Bishop Macarius spread the news. The Christian world rejoiced, and Emperor Constantine provided the means, and ordered the erection of a magnificent group of buildings over the "miraculously discovered site." These were completed, and dedicated on September 13, 335, in the presence of 300 bishops, and called the "Church of the Holy Sepulchre." In 333, when the church was yet incomplete, the Bordeaux Pilgrim described it as "a church of wondrous beauty."

This building stood until A.D. 614, when Chosroes II demolished and burned it. By popular subscription it was rebuilt, and stood until destroyed by the so-called "Mad Caliph Hakem" in 1010. Within 38 years it was rebuilt, and later taken over by the Crusaders when they entered Jerusalem in 1099. At once they set about the task of enlarging and beautifying the structure. This building stood until it was burned in the great fire in September of 1808. Three million dollars in subscriptions was received, and within two years another church arose over the site. The funds were not used as judiciously as they might have been, and so the building was not as beautiful nor as substantial as the former ones, yet it stands today, the pride and glory of Eastern Christians.

This church is 200 by 230 feet in size, and is sup-

The traditional place of Christ's burial within the Church of the Holy Sepulchre.

posed to cover both the hill where Christ was crucified and the tomb in which He was laid. The hill is 15 feet above the entrance to the church, and is reached by two flights of stone steps. A silver-lined cavity within the rock holds in place the gem-studded "true cross." The gems, jewels, and precious stones which ornament the cross are estimated to be worth more than $2 million.

On the entrance level, in the center of the rotunda under the great dome, is the Chapel of the Sepulchre, which is 26 feet long, 17 feet wide, and 15 feet high. It is built of white marble and resembles a small church with its columns and pilasters, and its immense candles and ornate decorations lavishly adorning its front.

The chapel has an anteroom with short stone benches where visitors sit to remove their shoes. Then comes the small Chapel of the Angels, which is just before the tomb where the angels are said to have rolled away the stone. A low, narrow doorway leads into the "holy of holies" of the entire structure—the Holy Sepulchre itself, which is six and one-half feet long by six feet wide. It contains 43 gold and silver lamps which are kept continually burning. On the right of the entrance, occupying nearly one-half of the floor space, is the tomb. This is covered with a large marble slab which is used for an altar where Mass is celebrated and where individuals bow in prayer.

Throughout the church are 37 stations at which worship is held—each one said to have been made sacred by some event connected with the crucifixion and burial of Christ.

There are many contrivances and inventions within this church, yet no place in the Christian world has been regarded with such awe and treated with such reverence as that occupied by the building known as the Church of the Holy Sepulchre. No place has been fought for and longed for as has this one. For more than 16 centuries the faces of European and Oriental Christians have been turned devoutly toward this traditional tomb. It has been estimated that from one-half to two-thirds of all Christendom love this place above all others because they believe the hillock to be Golgotha, and the sepulchre to be the one wherein their crucified Lord lay.

However, the location of the Church of the Holy Sepulchre is well within the walls of the present city. Some writers explain this by saying that at the time of the Crucifixion the present site was outside the walls, but that after Constantine had this church built, the city spread out and surrounded it. Others are equally certain that the present site must have been within the limits of the ancient city, and that we must look elsewhere for the true site of the Crucifixion. Many small excavations have been carried on to ascertain the exact location of the walls in this area during that period, but, as Dr. Kathleen Kenyon has well said, "The whole question requires further investigation."

Bezetha, the New City

Bezetha, the New City, lies north of the Temple area and much of it east of the upper reaches of the Tyropean Valley. In ancient times it was divided from the Temple area and the Tower of Antonia by a small valley, in which was formed a moat, or artificial cutting in the rock, 40 or more feet deep and more than 100 feet wide.

Josephus tells us that during the time of Herod Agrippa, when the city had grown more populous, "it gradually crept beyond its old limits and came to include this hill north of Moriah, which made the city of Jerusalem considerably larger."[37] A wall was thrown about the new part of the city, a deep moat was dug beyond the wall, and Jerusalem accommodated and gave security to more people. Thus Bezetha was apparently outside the second wall, but was included within the third wall.

84   The Pool of Bethesda (the "House of Mercy"), with

The Via Dolorosa (Way of the Cross), a narrow street in the Old City connecting the Tower of Antonia and the Church of the Holy Sepulchre.

its five porches, was in the southeastern portion of Bezetha. In fact some scholars suppose that the name Bethesda is derived from Bezetha.

While excavating just west of the present church of St. Ann, in 1871, the excavators went down some 60 feet below the present ground level and discovered an ancient pool (or twin pools) cut in the solid rock. Over this was the ruins of a building with a number of extensions which could be called "porches." And, too, it had a painting on one of the walls which pictured Christ healing the lame man. The structure was of Crusader origin, and was placed there by them because they fully believed this to be the Pool of Bethesda.

Through much of southern Bezetha and the North-west Hill runs the modern *Via Dolorosa* ("the Way of Sorrows") with its 14 "Stations of the Cross"—two in the Praetorium, seven in the street, and five in the Church of the Holy Sepulchre. Yet these are only representative, for Christ did not walk on the present street level, but on the true Roman level, which, on an average, is about 30 feet below the present level. Many houses and gardens in this area are supported on a series of vaults and arches, and under these are yet other structures which show up as the excavations deepen to the Roman level.

The Fortress of Antonia

This battlement, commonly known in New Testament times as "the castle," was built by Herod the Great and named Antonia in honor of Marcus Antonius (Mark Antony). It stood at the northwest corner of the Temple area, and was separated from Bezetha by the more ancient moat. Yet the tower was so near to Bezetha that it was said to adjoin the New City. At the same time, it had an underground passage to the Temple and steps leading down into the outer Temple courts. Here, on the steps of this "castle," Paul "stood . . . and beckoned with his hand unto the people," and spoke his defense to the Jerusalem mob.[38]

Some of the steps of the old castle, hewn partly into the solid rock, are still visible, but the site of the castle is occupied by the police barracks. Nearby, the tallest minaret of the Haram lifts its covered gallery high above the corner of the great Wall. Northward, where now stands the Convent of the Sisters of Zion, Father Ratisbon excavated in 1857-58 and found Roman arches of the time of Hadrian (A.D. 133), stone bullets used during the Roman siege of the city in A.D. 70, and Roman game markings on the street pavement of the time of Pilate. Here, it is assumed, the Roman guards at the Praetorium scratched the game outlines and played, in order to pass away the time.

CHAPTER 4

The Walls About Jerusalem

The far-famed city of Jerusalem, for almost 4,000 years—since at least the time of Abraham—has been a military stronghold with massive walls, imposing towers, and many gates. The Canaanite Jebusites enclosed the Ophel area with walls about 1800 B.C. David encountered these walls about 1000 B.C. and offered due reward to the first of his warriors who would mount them and make possible the defeat of the Jebu-

Air view of the walled part of the city of Jerusalem

sites.[1] Having captured Jerusalem for his capital, David united the Hebrews into a nation, rebuilt and extended the walls to the north, including a tower overlooking the City of David. Solomon extended the walls about Mount Moriah and, some think, about the Western Hill.[2]

Hezekiah "rebuilt" and repaired the walls about 700 B.C., only to have the Babylonians raze them in 586 B.C., along with the Temple. On returning from Babylon in 536 B.C., the Israelites rebuilt the Temple in a less pretentious way, but seemed to do little about the walls. Forty years afterwards, Nehemiah arrived to restore the walls which still were "broken down." After his famous night ride about these walls, he and others rebuilt the walls with a trowel in one hand and a sword in the other.[8]

Time after time the walls were destroyed and again rebuilt, both before and after the lifetime of Jesus. Not always were they rebuilt in the same place, nor did they always encompass the same area. In Jerusalem's earliest period, its walls may not have taken in more than 11 to 13 acres. In Herod's day they probably enclosed some 350 acres; and with the building of Hadrian's "third wall," they must have covered considerably more than half of the 1,000-acre plateau formed by the five hills.

The present massive light brown, pale pink, and gray walls enclose only 210 acres, but with their broad gates and flanking towers they give the old city of Jerusalem the appearance of a great fortress of the Middle Ages. It merits the designation as the world's most excellently walled and gated city. These outside walls, built mostly by Suleiman the Magnificent in 1538-42, are from four to 14 feet thick, and vary in height from 30 to 50 feet above the outside ground level.

The inside Temple walls—for the most part, built earlier—are sometimes higher, and are usually more massive. At the famous southeast corner of the Temple area, the wall is nearly 80 feet above the outside ground, and from excavations we know it descends more than 90 feet below the present ground level.

The average height of the old city wall is 38 feet. It is two and a half miles long, and forms a rough square, with the four sides facing the cardinal points of the compass. The masonry presents a mosaic of stonecutting art, a veritable study in archaeology itself, a symbol of the city's turbulent history. The huge foundation stones speak of the time of Herod and of Jesus, while the smooth-faced, squared, small upper courses are clearly Moslem and Turkish.

These walls are pierced by seven open gates, supported by 34 strong towers, and have parapets along the top on which medieval defending forces could move about easily. Today it is a unique experience to mount these walls and walk around the Holy City, viewing it and its environs from the many angles.

Attempts to identify and trace the walls which surrounded ancient Jerusalem have intrigued archaeologists for more than a century. Nearly a quarter of a million dollars, many years of time, and much noble effort have gone into the search. Such names as Robinson, Warren, Wilson, Conder, Bliss, A. C. Dickie, Raymond Weill, R. A. S. Macalister, L. A. Meyer, J. B. Hennessy, Kathleen Kenyon, W. F. Stinesprings, and Benjamin Mazar have ranked high in the work. More recent excavators have benefited from the more precise understanding of archaeology as well as from the actual work of the pioneers. Yet it is still a complicated task, for there have been many walls during the long history of destruction, rebuilding, and expansion of Jerusalem as its fate has waxed and waned through the ages—Canaanite, Davidic, Solomonic, Nehemian, Maccabean, Herodian, Agrippian, Hadrian, Eudocian, Crusader, Turkish, Arabic, and even British. It leaves the uninitiated seeing merely walls, and the specialist often uncertain about what he sees.[4]

From the appearance of the east, south, and west walls about the Temple area, it was long assumed that at least their lower courses of large, fine stones had some connection with the ancient walls. Also their locations were suggestive, for this eastern wall of the Temple grounds follows along the edge of the deep Kidron Valley, the western wall is along the edge of the Tyropoeon Valley, while the southern wall forms the boundary line of the Temple grounds with the ancient City of David. It was believed, therefore, that these three walls must be more or less along the course of the ancient walls.

The Western Walls

With the above assumptions in mind, Dr. Edward Robinson (in 1838) was inspecting the stones in the 1600-

foot-long western wall. Near the southwest corner, he found that the corner stone next above the surface of the ground "measured thirty feet, ten inches in length by six and one-half feet broad; and several others varied from twenty and one-half to twenty-four and one-half feet long by five feet in thickness."[5] But the discovery which interested him most was three courses of large stones, hewn to a curve, 51 feet wide and projecting several feet out from the wall. This foundation suggested to him the eastern part of an immense arch which may have supported a *bridge,* which in Herod's time spanned the Tyropoeon Valley (now filled with debris to a depth of about 60 to 80 feet) and connected this part of the Temple area with the much higher Western Hill across the valley. Robinson's assumptions were subsequently verified, and the arch became known as Robinson's Arch.

Sir Charles Wilson discovered another arch springing from this same western wall, but 560 feet north of Robinson's Arch. It had the same span as Robinson's Arch, although more complete, since there were 25 courses of stone—12 on each side of the keystone. This, too, formed a part of another bridge across the Tyropoeon Valley that connected the Temple with the Western Hill, or Upper City, usually called Mount Zion. The outer court of the Temple, according to Josephus, had been entered on the western or city side by four gates, the two principal ones being at the points indicated by Robinson's Arch and Wilson's Arch.[6]

At three places shafts were sunk, and the lower courses of this wall were checked—at Robinson's Arch, at the Wailing Wall, and at Wilson's Arch. At each, the wall was found to continue downward from 65 to 80 feet below the present ground or pavement level. It was constructed of bevelled-edged and beautifully cut Herodian masonry, except the very lowest courses of stone, which were hammer-dressed and impressed the excavators as possibly hav-

92

Southeast corner of the Temple Area wall, which is also the corner of the city wall. Here Warren found the huge cornerstone 93 feet below the present ground level.

ing been laid by Solomon.[7] The longest stone yet found in Jerusalem's walls is a huge one near the southwest corner of the Temple area. It measures 38 ft. 9 in., but is only about 3 ft. 6 in. in height and lies between Robinson's Arch and the Wailing Wall. It was near this southwest corner, under an ancient pavement 22 feet below the present ground level, that they uncovered the black stone signet "of Haggai, the son of Shebaniah," bringing to memory the prophet Haggai, who labored to rebuild the temple in 520 B.C.[8]

Sir Charles Warren sank three shafts at varying distances from the famous southeast corner of the Temple wall: one 90 feet, another 100 feet, and one 125 feet below the ground level. At various intervals, horizontal galleries were tunneled across to the walls and careful inspections made. The masonry had been laid in courses of varying heights with a precision and fineness of joint surpassed only by the early Egyptian work on the pyramids. The stones in some of the lower courses bore quarry marks which were thought by some to be Phoenician characters possibly placed there by one of King Hiram's overseers who aided Solomon. However, the major portion of the wall was clearly of Herodian masonry, laid there by Herod the Great just a few years before the birth of Jesus.

Near the corner, more than 90 feet below ground level, Warren discovered a large stone, 3 ft. 8 in. tall by 14 ft. long that weighed approximately 100 tons. It had been finely dressed and apparently set in place as "the chief corner stone"—not of the Temple itself, but of the great city wall enclosing the sacred Temple area.[9]

In his efforts to trace the ancient city walls, Warren sank eight shafts on the Hill Ophel, south of the present east city wall, and laid bare more than 400 feet of what he thought to be David's Wall. When the wall abruptly ended, and he could find no further extension, he concluded that the missing portion of the wall "had been taken up and sold for building stone." In commenting on this common practice, he said:

> "Cut stone in Jerusalem is much in demand, and on the gounds of the fellahin all traces of walls at or near the surface are fast disappearing. The rock-cut steps and caves which existed along the slopes of Ophel are also fast becoming obliterated: the farmers find these are the places where they have least trouble in blasting and quarrying rock, and within the last few years many old features of the southern side of the old city have vanished; thus, year by year, old Jerusalem will become most difficult to be understood.[10]

Many others have gone wall-hunting—along with their royal-tomb hunts—here on Ophel, the City of David. But the most expensive, the most extended, and in some respects the most thorough search was made in 1961-62 by Dr. Kathleen Kenyon, director of the British School of Archaeology in Jerusalem. With a splendid force of helpers, and with the avowed purpose of locating the east wall of the original Jebusite town of Jerusalem, she began well up on the summit of Ophel, and cut a 36-foot-wide trench down the eastern slope of the mound toward the Virgin's Fountain (Gihon), ancient Jerusalem's main water supply.

Near the brow of the hill she uncovered the foundations of a Maccabean Wall. Farther down the slope there appeared massive stone buildings, along with pottery of the seventh century B.C. Then, when more than two-thirds of the way down, she came upon a wall of large hewn stones, against which there was "a filling containing only Middle Bronze Age pottery." The eastern base of the wall was only about 65 feet from the Virgin's Fountain, and clearly dated to "about 1800 B.C." Her conclusion was that here was the Jebusite wall of east Jerusalem, and that this particular section "remained the town wall under David," and continued until the beginning of the seventh century B.C., "when it was superseded by a wall that crossed its top."[11]

Between 1893 and 1897, Frederick J. Bliss and A. C. Dickie traced and uncovered an ancient wall which started near the Pool of Siloam and encircled the brow of the Western Hill along the Hinnom Valley side, then turned northward by Bishop Gobat School and the Protestant Cemetery to join the present city wall at the southwest corner. There was revealed a splendid wall about this fine, imposing Western Hill. But when and by whom was the wall constructed? Bliss dated it as early as Solomon, and Kathleen Kenyon as late as Herod Agrippa.

Another wall long since quarried away for its building stone, or a wall as yet undiscovered, could well have enclosed this Western Hill at an earlier period. Careful scholarship dare not speak here with a note of finality when, archaeologically, there is only negative evidence. Other places where we know that once there were walls have none now—no stones survive, nor are there signs of walls having ever been on the portions excavated thus far. This could very well be the situation here, seeing that the literary evidences for an early wall here are very good. Solomon is not only said to have "repaired the breaches of the city of David his father," but also to have built "the wall of Jerusalem round about" (I Kings 3:1; 9:15; 11:27). Evidently "the wall of Jerusalem round about" was intended to mean something other than a wall about Ophel and Moriah. Good men through the ages have taken it to mean also a wall about the Upper City—the Western Hill.

Also, the biblical record tells us very plainly that King Hezekiah tunneled under the Hill Ophel and brought the water from Gihon spring *into* the city, so it would be within the city wall and therefore inaccessible to the coming enemy. This was the whole thought and intent of Hezekiah's plan and project—that the new reservoir of water would be *within* the city's defenses or fortifications. The end of the tunnel, the stone-carved inscription giving a detailed account of the engineering project, and the ruined pool remain to our day in the Tyropoeon Valley. Therefore, for the pool to be *within* the city of Hezekiah's day, (701 B.C.) it would have been necessary for a city wall of defense to cross the Tyropoeon Valley and to encircle at least a considerable portion of the Western Hill. No amount of explaining can make it otherwise. The chances are very good that Solomon placed that wall of defense there about 250 years before Hezekiah's time.

The North Walls

Josephus describes three successive north walls which Titus had to breach before he could reach the Temple. The first wall, as most agree, ran east from the Jaffa Gate to the Gate of the Chain near the middle of the west Temple wall—nearly parallel to the present David's Street and its extension which is known as The Street of the Chain.

The second wall, we are told, "took its beginning from the gate which was called Gannath," and after encompassing the northern part of the city, came back to the Tower of Antonia. The precise course of this wall is uncertain. But many believe portions of this second wall to have been along the line of the present North Wall— especially in the vicinity of Damascus Gate. The alternative line, which some have drawn for this wall, would have encompassed much too small an area, especially when much of it would have been taken up by the Tyropoeon Valley. And, too, its course would have run almost entirely on low ground, leaving the higher ground and the hills immediately outside. According to military judgment this would have been rather poor planning.[12]

To provide greater protection to Jerusalem from the north, King Herod Agrippa I (A.D. 40-44) added the Third Wall as his major physical contribution to Jerusalem. Josephus says this wall began "at the Tower of Hippicus" (probably the present "David's Tower") and went north-

west to the Tower of Psephinus (thought to have been recently located 1,000 yards northwest of David's Tower under the building of the Brethren of the Christian Schools). From there it ran northeast "over against the monuments of Helena, queen of Abiabene" (the present Tombs of the Kings) and "the sepulchral caverns of the Kings," then southward back to the eastern Temple wall.[13]

Traces of what was thought to be the Third Wall mentioned by Josephus were noticed by Robinson when he was in Jerusalem in 1838, and by others before him and many since. Among them are Selah Merrill, United States consul, and L. B. Paton, director of the American School of Oriental Research, in 1903-4. But so many of its stones had been carried away for other construction that many people had come to wonder whether these men had seen actual wall remnants. Then, in 1925, when repairs were being made on the Nablus road, directly west of the American School of Oriental Research, a most impressive wall with magnificent stones "of distinctly Herodian type" was revealed. The Department of Antiquities cleared the stones, surrounded them by a rail, and left them exposed.[14]

Challenged by this ancient wall section, E. L. Sukenik and L. A. Meyer of the Hebrew University at Jerusalem obtained a permit and excavated the wall at several points along the line indicated by the position of the stones. In 1926 Professor Romain, of the American School of Oriental Research, discovered that road repairs had partially uncovered great stones forming portions of a tower and gate in front of the school property. He notified Sukenik and together they excavated the area, which extended about 26 feet onto the school property.

In 1940, more evidence of the road showed up at the northeast corner of the school property when Sukenik and Meyer excavated and uncovered foundations of a great tower that were 43 feet wide and extended back under the tennis court. Other portions of the wall were found

he once heavily fortified North Wall, which at first had a
0-foot moat, now filled in, along which the roadway runs.

on the school property in 1942, and still another section in 1959.

More remnants of the wall and the foundations of a large tower were later located a considerable distance east of the school grounds. Then, apparently, the wall turned south until it connected with the present wall near the northeast corner of the Old City.[15] All these wall locations fell in line with Josephus' statement ("Wars," V, 7:3) that, after the capture of the third or outer wall, Titus moved his camp within the wall, thus "occupying all the intervening space as far as the Kedron, but keeping a sufficient distance away from the second wall as to be out of range of missles."

These excavations satisfied many as identifying the line of the "third wall," but more recent excavations by J. B. Hennessy, of the British School, below and around the Damascus Gate revealed remnants of a more ancient gate and arch which Kathleen Kenyon and some others are convinced were constructed by Herod Agrippa I. They favor the view, therefore, that the course of Agrippa's wall was that followed essentially by today's Northern Wall. Other archaeologists, however, continue to hold that Agrippa's wall lay much farther north—most probably that uncovered by Sukenik and Meyer, some 400 yards north of the present wall. At least, it more precisely fits the description and location as given by Josephus. And Josephus is the one historian who was thoroughly acquainted with the course of this wall, having seen it *many* times as he came up to Jerusalem. He was also present throughout the siege of the city by Titus in A.D. 70.

With a determined effort to unlock more of the wonderful secrets of the ancient walls, Professor Benjamin Mazar and his associates of the Hebrew University—involving as many as 120 volunteers from Israel and other countries—began a long-term archaeological expedition in Jerusalem in February, 1968. By the end of the first year

Courses of Herodian stone in the southern wall of the Temple area recently uncovered by Dr. Benjamin Mazar Some of the stones weigh 80 to 100 tons each.

they had (1) exposed the foundation walls of Robinson's Arch and further confirmed the theory that the arch is the relic of the southern of two bridges leading across the Tyropoeon Valley from the Upper City on Mt. Zion to the Temple Hill, upon which Herod and his retinue walked to the Temple from his palace; (2) found many coins and clay vessels, one of which was inscribed with the Hebrew word "Korban" (burnt offering), which was probably a Temple vessel; and (3) uncovered 19 courses of the Western Wall, and 14 of the Southern Wall, reaching down to the Herodian pavement. Some of the stones in the wall weighed 80 to 100 tons. Now comes the news that he has discovered remnants of the walls which Nehemiah rebuilt.

THE CITADEL OR TOWER OF DAVID

The most ancient, the most massive, and the most imposing building within the walls of the ancient city of Jerusalem is the Citadel or Tower of David. It stands immediately south of the Jaffa Gate, and is usually the first of the ancient public buildings that catches the eye of a visitor or pilgrim to the Holy City.

It is an irregular group of five square towers, all constituting one fortification, and surrounded by a moat. The moat is about 30 feet wide at the top, and where it has not been filled up to some extent, it is about 20 feet deep. It is walled on the outer side, and this wall rises about three feet above the surface to prevent persons and beasts from falling into the moat. The moat, before much of it was filled, was 460 feet long on the western side, which is outside the city, and was nearly as long on the eastern side. On the other two sides it is about half as long. From the bottom of the moat, on its inner side, the foundation wall of the tower rises at an angle of about 45 degrees, until it reaches the level of the exterior surface, but the upper wall resting on this is vertical. The height of the entire structure is about 80 feet.

David's Tower, located near the Jaffa Gate, and sometimes called "The Citadel of Zion," dates back to the days of Herod.

The foundation wall is built of very large and very ancient-looking stones, many of them eight or 10 feet long and three feet thick. These, with their marginal drafts of from four to five inches wide, are certainly as old as Herod the Great, but could be even older.[16] This is especially 103 true of the northeastern variety of stones, with the bevelled edges, and apparently occupying their original places.

This venerable structure, known since early Crusader times as the Tower of David, is the finest of its kind to be found in Palestine. Its name awakens many memories of Israel's colorful king, yet many think it cannot rightfully be regarded as being the "strong tower of David," of which the writer of the Song of Solomon spoke: "Thy neck is like the tower of David builded for an armoury, whereon there hang a thousand bucklers, all shields of mighty men" (Song of Sol. 4:4).

However, it is universally acknowledged that this portion of the Western Hill was covered in part, or perhaps entirely, by Herod's Upper Palace, with its gardens, and by the three towers of Phasaelus, Hippicus, and Mariamne, which adjoined it on the north. Josephus has left us a glowing account of the royal palace, which "was entirely surrounded by a wall thirty cubits high, with decorated towers at equal intervals, and contained enormous banqueting halls, besides numerous chambers richly adorned." [17]

The towers were built of blocks of white marble of great size, "so exactly joined together that each tower appeared to be one mass of rock." They played a prominent part during the memorable siege by the Romans. These three towers were left standing by Titus when he destroyed the city, to protect the legion left to garrison the place and to prevent any insurrectionary movements on the part of the Jews.

The lower masonry of the present structure is of great antiquity. It is generally agreed by the best authorities that these huge, yellowed stones at the base of the tower, and the part of this structure which is below the present ground level, were constructed by Herod the Great and stood in the time of Jesus Christ. However, the major portion of these remains which belong to Herod's Palace are buried beneath a mass of rubble more than 30 feet deep. Some stones in the structure are earlier than Herod; others are much later.

The Citadel, as we now know it, was remodeled in the fourteenth century, and again repaired in the sixteenth century. With its five square towers and other buildings, surrounded by a ditch, it must have presented a commanding position. Before the introduction of firearms it would be of great strength.

The escarp retains to some extent its original appearance, but time, hard treatment, and earthquakes have worn away or dislocated much of the finer work. Furthermore, the repairs carried out by the Turks were executed in a rather slovenly manner. Those which were done by the British in 1929, at a cost of some $30,000, were better. The old stonework, where it can be seen, is equal to the best specimens of masonry in the famous southeast wall surrounding the Temple platform. The faces of the stones are dressed with an astonishing degree of fineness, and the whole, when perfect, must have presented a smooth surface difficult to ascend, and probably unassailable by the battering ram.

The superstructure of the Citadel contains several rooms and a cistern for the collection of rainwater. In one of the rooms, a "mihrab" marks the place where, according to Moslem tradition, David composed the psalms, and another room is pointed out as the reception room of the king.

The Tower of David was the last place to yield when Jerusalem was captured by the Crusaders. And when the city walls were destroyed by the Moslems in the thirteenth century, the Citadel was spared, "to come down to our own time as a fine example of the mural masonry of the Jews."

From the steps of David's Tower, on December 11,   105

1917, General Allenby read his proclamation in English, French, Italian, Arabic, and Hebrew, announcing peace and toleration for all races and creeds within the Holy City. Representatives of many governments were present, along with many prominent people—including Lowell Thomas. Afterwards, the British transformed the edifice into a museum for curios and antiquities.

Now the question has arisen from time to time: Was David's Tower, or Citadel, ever located here, or even in this area? Josephus, most authentic Jewish historian of the first century A.D., does cite the tradition that this Western Hill was called "the Citadel" by King David, and in this tradition he rather faintly concurs.[18]

However, recent scholarship, for the most part, takes the position that David's fortifications were on Mount Ophel—at least most of them. Since buildings cover the greater part of the Western Hill at the present time, we will probably not have a final answer from archaeological research for some time to come—if ever. There is always the possibility that Josephus could be right—that David had a second "citadel" as a fortification for this "Upper Jerusalem."

THE WAILING WALL

This grim, gray, hyssop-tufted, architectural fragment known as the Wailing Wall, towers about 57 to 60 feet above what was once a narrow, 90-foot-long, stone-paved courtyard (since widened) just on the border line between the west side of the Temple area and the city proper.

Its five lower courses are made up of huge, marginal-drafted stones, which, according to archaeological methods of reckoning, identify them as Herodian masonry. That is, they were carved at least as early as during the first cen-

The Western Wall of the Temple area, called the Wailing Wall, one of the most sacred Jewish sites.

tury before Christ. Above them are four courses of ancient masonry whose margins are undrafted. These are Roman work—cut sometime during the first centuries after Christ. The upper courses, which are of smaller blocks, are Arab work of the Middle Ages.

Some of the stones in the lower portion of this grand old wall are as large as 16½ feet long by 13 feet wide, and are so old and so strikingly beautiful that they are regarded as some of the world's finest and most venerable stones. There is good reason to believe they once formed some part of Herod's Temple, or at least the outermost wall and portico which surrounded the Temple and enclosed the Court of the Gentiles.

Evidently most of these older stones which we now see above the ground level were thrown down with the destruction of Jerusalem by Titus in A.D. 70 and later were picked up in this area and laid in the wall, thus giving substance to Christ's prophecy, "There shall not be left here one stone upon another that shall not be thrown down." However, the lower course of stone in this wall appears to be in its original position. And it is a part of a wall that extends down about 70 feet below these lowest stones which we now see.

Jewish tradition holds that this portion of the Western Wall is the one remnant left of the "containing wall of the outermost enclosures of Herod's Temple" that has survived the destruction of war and of the elements. Many are confident that when God's Shekinah presence left the holy of holies of the Temple, at its destruction, the Divine Presence went to this section of the Western Wall and hovers over it to this day. Orthodox Jews, along with many others, have not only thoroughly believed this but through the many centuries have felt this to be the nearest they might approach to the holy of holies. Therefore, from at least as far back as the time of the Bordeaux Pilgrim (A.D. 333), Jews of nearly all types have gathered here from all parts of the world for prayers. This is especially true on the eve of their Sabbaths (Fridays at sunset), on feast days, and on other special occasions such as the Day of Atonement. Thousands who cannot pray at this wall in Jerusalem send money to have others pray there for them.

At times the prayers are led by a minister who chants a line, and the people respond with quotations from the Psalms and Lamentations as they mourn "the Temple that is destroyed" and "the majesty that is departed" from Israel. At other times they pray individual prayers, which may be for the forgiveness of their sins, for the healing of a loved one who is very ill, or for any other need they might have. Neither light thoughts nor jests are engaged in by the Jews at the Wailing Wall, for this is the most sacred site or "holy place" they have had through the centuries since their Temple was destroyed. Even in medieval times it was sometimes called the Gate of Mercy.[19] And when they meet there, it is in reality not to worship some relic, but to pray in deep earnestness and devotion to Almighty God. Therefore their prayers are as varied as human needs and devotions.

The Jews were shut out from this, their most sacred place of prayer, for 19 years—from 1948 to 1967. During that time, no Jew was permitted near the Wailing Wall—not even near the walls of old Jerusalem, which was the Arab section of the divided city. For them, their only consolation lay in the fact that they were in possession of a large portion of Palestine. This they believed to be an answer to their prayers. Yet their deepest yearning was to return to this Western Wall for prayer.

On June 6, 1967, when the Israeli army was recapturing ancient Jerusalem, their first act was to take the Temple Mount, then to march straight for the Western Wall. Near the narrow entrance to the wall stood Arab legionnaires, their hands raised in surrender. The first Israeli soldier through shouted: "The Western Wall! I can see the

Looking towards the Wailing Wall across the open area created by the recent removal of a large number of old buildings.

Wall," and "then the rest rushed through to touch and kiss the hallowed stones. Tough paratroopers, who had fought hard and non-stop for thirty-two hours, wept at the Temple wall over which their people had wailed for so many centuries."[20] Soon there came a jeep bearing Brigadier General Rabbi Shlomo Goren, chief chaplain to the Israeli forces. The rabbi jumped from the jeep and rushed down the lane to the Western Wall, where he offered a Hebrew prayer, then "drawing forth a shofar, normally sounded only on the most solemn of Jewish holy days, he blew a long and powerful blast."[21] Soon afterwards came General Moshe Dayan, General Rabin, Prime Minister Eshkol, followed by other members of the Cabinet—all to pray with rejoicing and thanksgiving to Jehovah that He had brought them again to their most sacred holy place. Faith had become a reality, and the joy of thousands knew no bounds as they hurried to the Wall. The scene was considered of sufficient significance that broadcasting companies radioed and televised it to the world.

Within a short time the Israeli Government cleared away the old, poorly constructed buildings which stood near the Wall and lowered the ground level to reveal still one more course of ancient stones. Then they paved the extended area and made it convenient for large crowds to gather here for prayer—as in ancient times they gathered in the Temple courts to pray.

On the festival of the Feast of Weeks, which occurred on Wednesday, June 14 (exactly one week after Jerusalem was united), 200,000 Jews from all parts of the country paid homage at the Western Wall. On a day-by-day basis, it is still the most frequented place in the Holy City. The crowds are especially large on Friday afternoons (the eve of the Jewish Sabbath) and on special holy days.

CHAPTER 5

The City Gates and Streets

In ancient and medieval times, most important cities were enclosed by substantial walls. These walls were pierced by fortified gates through which the people could come and go but which could be closed against enemies. In some cities, such as Jericho, there was but one gate, but most had several gates. Ezekiel and John pictured the ideal city as having 12 gates—three toward each of the cardinal points of the compass.[1]

The ponderous doors with which the city gates were shut were made of heavy material and covered with bronze or some other metal. They were secured with bronze (brass) or iron bars and bolts.[2] They were closed at night or during war, and at times on the Sabbath.[3] Some gates had a small door cut into the large door, which by some was called "the needle's eye." Through this the belated traveler, who could give a satisfactory account of himself to the sentry, could be admitted.

A tower was usually built over and about the gate-

Street scene inside the Damascus Gate

way, along with two or more guardrooms. Here a sentinel kept watch in order to announce approaching danger. Some important gates had two towers, usually 20 to 30 feet square, which projected beyond the wall. These larger gates had more guardrooms. Some were, as usual, used to accommodate the guards, but others served as courtrooms where sat the judge or "the elders" to hear court cases, administer "justice in the gates," and witness the sealing of contracts.[4]

Near the gates, both within and without the city, were open spaces where the people bought and sold, and heard announcements during the day. Here also strangers and country dwellers who had no better accommodations wrapped themselves in their *abayas* (cloaks or long outer coats) and slept for the night. When a city fell or was captured, the victorious king or conqueror often sat at, or near, the principal gate to receive the officers and leaders of the capitulating city, specify terms, and give directions for the disposal of both the booty and the captives. A graphic picture of such an incident is seen in the Nineveh bas-relief on the walls of Sennacherib's palace, where the king is shown sitting on his temporary throne at the principal gate of Lachish as the city is surrendered to him.

The pageantry of the everyday life of an Oriental city may be seen best at its gates—especially at one of the chief gates of old Jerusalem, the world's richest and best example of a medieval Moslem city. Here the money changer sits at his glass-covered money table in eager readiness to change your money (for a price!). Nearby, the scribe with his writing equipment waits to oblige those who need his services. Somewhat farther away is the chauffeur, who waits to take you places, and the man with the small pyramids of grain, who is ready to give you (hopefully) "good measure, pressed down, and shaken together, and running over."

But those passing through the gate present a moving

panorama of many elements very much like those of Bible times: stately Bedouin Arabs dressed in colorful robes and wearing flowing headgear and bearing themselves like the lords of the land; fine-faced, old patriarchs, well-shaped and masterful like the Moses of Michelangelo; orthodox rabbis arrayed in tall, furry headgear and long, dark coats prescribed by the Talmud; pale young Poles in fur-trimmed hats, trailing robes, and corkscrew curls dangling over their temples; priests, nuns, and teaching sisters variously clothed in the sombre garbs of their orders; Martha-like Arab women dressed in vivid colors and bearing on their heads mountains of cauliflower; the wizened Yemenite porters bent beneath stacks of crates; donkeys staggering under the loads of produce; and an occasional camel laden with dates, sesame seed, or other supplies for the nearby markets. Seldom is the Westerner without a worthwhile scene as he lingers about any one of the principal gates of Jerusalem.

THE JAFFA GATE

In giving consideration to the gates of present Jerusalem, we begin with Jaffa Gate, which the Arabs call *Bab al-Khalil*—the "Gate of the Friend." It is so named from the fact that a roadway from it leads to the city of Hebron, where dwelt Abraham, "the Friend of God." The name Jaffa is but the Arabic rendering of Joppa, the coastal city to which a second road leads westward. Thus the gate stands at the junction of two main roads, the one to Bethlehem, Hebron, and Beersheba; the other to Ramleh and Jaffa.

It is of castle-like construction which attains a height of about 50 feet. The battlemented top would have suggested military strength to men of medieval times, but it is not strong enough to bear modern guns of even the lightest caliber.

The front of the gate is about 40 feet across in all and   115

the sides about 18 feet deep. The entrance, from the city side, is through a comparatively narrow gate, which fits roughly into the lower part of a high, pointed arch, filled in with masonry above and at the sides to suit the present door. In the bow of the arch, about 20 feet above the ground, is an inscription in Arabic mentioning Suleiman "the Magnificent," and on the door itself are found a star and a crescent, emblems of the Mohammedan faith. About halfway through Jaffa Gate, as in many other similar gates, there is a right-angled turn which in earlier times was of great aid to the defenders of the city. This is known as the indirect-access type of city gate.

It was outside Jaffa Gate, in A.D. 637, after his armies had conquered and taken charge of the city for the Arabs, that Caliph Omar dismounted from his red camel, pitched his tent, calmly seated himself on the ground, signed the capitulation, ate his frugal meal of nuts and dates, then remounted and rode his camel through this gate into the Holy City. Later it was required that pilgrims enter Jerusalem only through Jaffa Gate.

In 1898, Kaiser Wilhelm of Germany realized his long cherished desire to visit the Holy Land in person. Desiring to enter the city of Jerusalem, not as a mere Prussian monarch, nor even as a pilgrim, but as a medieval knight such as Godfrey de Bouillon or Baldwin I, he initiated plans which would permit him to make his entry in the nature of a symbolical triumph. For the better display of this spectacle, a 50-foot portion of the old wall between David's Tower and Jaffa Gate was demolished and a new entrance road made for the Kaiser. Clothed in white garments and wearing a crown of gold on his head, he rode through this opening into the city on a pure white Arabian stallion. In symbol, the pageant represented his taking possession of the Holy City.

In striking contrast to this, General Allenby, the great British general who captured Jerusalem from the Turks, on 117

The Jaffa Gate

December 9, 1917, planned his entry in simplicity. Showing alike his humility and his desire to pay respect to a historic city, long made sacred from religious associations, he entered on foot through Jaffa Gate. He refused to make use of the broad, paved thoroughfare prepared 19 years before by the order of the Kaiser. This modest, yet fearless entry was in harmony with the spirit of the prophets of old. The name Allenby fell upon the ears of the inhabitants of Jerusalem with singular force. To them it sounded like the blending of the Arabic words *Allah* (God) and *Neby* (Prophet)—the prophet of God. To the people he was the twentieth-century prophet of God sent to deliver them from the Turkish yoke. Jewish and Arab joy knew no bounds.

A clock tower of modern design was erected on the old tower of Jaffa Gate in 1907. Its dials indicated both European and Arabic hours, but it was soon considered out of harmony with the environs. It was therefore removed, leaving the gate to appear in its simple, medieval form.

During the latter part of the nineteenth century and up to Allenby's entry, Jaffa Gate was the only one which was not kept locked from dusk to sunrise. Only a sentry stood guard here.

In 1948 this gate was closed—including the nearby 40-foot wall opening—because it was on the border between the Israeli and Arab sections of Jerusalem. With the war of 1967, however, it was thrown open, and again became a principal gate of Jerusalem.

THE NEW GATE

Traveling clockwise from Jaffa Gate around the city walls, one comes to the northwest corner, near Allenby Square, and on turning eastward soon arrives at the New Gate, known by the Arabs as *Bab es Sultan Abdul Hamid*.

Abdul Hamid II ruled the Turkish Empire from 1876 to 1908, and brought a small measure of progress to Jeru-

salem. During the year 1889, at the request of interested citizens, he opened this New Gate to give ready access to Christian pilgrims and to the population living immediately outside the northwestern walls who desired to visit the Church of the Holy Sepulchre.

The New Gate has no tower, and no turn within its interior. It is merely a stone-framed opening, of simple architectural design, that offers passageway to the people. But it is a much used gate, and many are made to wonder how the people got along without it before it was opened. Jeremiah mentions a "new gate" in his day, but it was in the Temple.

During the Arab-Jewish division of 1948-67, this gate was blocked up with a barrier of stone and concrete, but it is now open for passage.

THE DAMASCUS GATE

The third gate is the Damascus Gate, so called because the road that leads north from it ultimately reaches Damascus. This name, however, is rather modern. The older name, as understood by the Arabs, is *Bab al-'Amoud,* or the Gate of the Column, from the single column which, in the Roman period, stood in the square just inside the gate. From this the Romans measured the distance from Jerusalem to other places in Palestine. Also a street of columns ran from this gate across the city to Zion's Gate, as appears so prominently on the sixth-century Madeba mosaic map of Jerusalem. Some fragments of these columns, a molded gate-front 10 feet high, and a portion of a paved street leading toward the gate were found by workmen during the year 1888. This portion of paved street was 23 feet below the present ground level.

A reservoir and a fragment of an ancient wall have been excavated close by and underneath the present gate. There still exist subterranean chambers of unknown age. These topographical and archaeological researches confirm the opinion that there was at this point, 23 feet below the present ground level, a city wall and gateway at least as ancient as the time of Herod the Great.

The time-stained, dull brown, light gray, and pale pink of the Damascus Gate is very impressive. Some of the lower stones measure seven feet long and four feet broad, and are drafted with the beveled edge similar to those in the Wailing Wall. This shows them to have been quarried at least as far back as the time of Herod the Great. However, they are not in their original location, but have been moved here and used with more modern stones for the construction of the more recent gate.

Damascus Gate stands astride the upper reaches of the Tyropoeon Valley, where the city has had the least natural protection, and hence the best man-made fortifica-

The Damascus Gate

tions. It is 50 feet high, and is the most elaborately constructed of all the present open gates. The gate is massive, yet graceful. Its arched entrance is set in a broad front, surrounded by adornments, and flanked on either side by a great tower. Carved above its arch are these words: "There is no God but God and Mohammed is His Prophet." The entire exterior of the gate-complex is topped by pinnacled battlements, and its interior passageway so effectively staggered and vaulted as to leave lasting impressions on one who passes through even once. There are steps inside the city which lead to the top of the nearby wall. This makes it the place where many start their walk around the top of the walls of the Holy City.

The Damascus Gate is the meeting place of four roads, and it could be that through the gate which once stood on this spot our Lord bore His cross to the lone, gray hill just outside which is thought by many to be Golgotha, "The Place of the Skull." At least the rocky face of the nearby hill bears the resemblance of a large skull. It was probably through this gate also that St. Paul started on the journey to Damascus, near the end of which he experienced his marvelous conversion.

In more recent times, outside the Damascus Gate, there has been built a beautiful hospice, dedicated to St. Paul, called the Lazarist Hospice. For a time it served as a residence for the German pastor in Jerusalem, and was the place where Kaiser Wilhem of Germany resided during his spectacular visit to the Holy City in 1898. Later it was used as a home for the Governorate, and then as an office building for the government of Palestine.

Today, as in past centuries, grain which is brought in from the Plain of Sharon, the Jordan Valley, and the fertile plains of Transjordan, is bought and sold by the merchants outside Damascus Gate. Arabs from the villages who have traveled a distance and entered the city during the day will often be seen, wrapped in their *abayas*, sleeping about the gate during the night.

The architectural beauty of this grand entrance, with its flanking towers, its battlements and its turrets, has caused many tourists to consider it to be the most striking of all the city gates. Certainly this old gateway with its time-stained stones, its interesting construction, and its unique position makes an impression that one never can, nor cares to, forget.

HEROD'S GATE

The fourth gate is Herod's Gate, known to the Arabs as *Bab es Zahirah*, which means "the Gate of Flowers." It forms the opening for foot traffic to and from the Bezetha section of Jerusalem. It would seem that the name of Herod, as associated with this gate, comes from a tradition that near this gate stood the house or palace of Herod Antipas. It was he who, with his men of war, rebuffed Jesus and mocked Him when Pilate sent Him to Herod for examination.

However, this gate could as properly be called the Gate of the Sheep Market, seeing that there was in ancient times a gate in a relative position in the north Temple wall which was known as the Sheep Gate. Even today, sheep and goats are brought here in large numbers to be bargained for by the butchers and other interested parties. Many authorities accept this as at least being relatively near the Sheep Gate of ancient times.

Large bunches of tall stalks of sugarcane are often seen leaning against the outside wall of the gate. These and other merchandise are offered for sale to those who care to buy. Considerable business is conducted at Herod's Gate, but on the whole it is a quiet place, because it is used for pedestrians only. The only wheel traffic in the vicinity passes along a nearby road outside the city.   123

St. Stephen's Gate

The fifth gate is St. Stephen's Gate, reputed to be near the site where the saintly Stephen was stoned to death by the enraged Jews, among whom was Saul of Tarsus. The Arabs also know it as *Bab Sitti Miriam* or "the Gate of Lady Mary," due to the fact that it leads to the church of the Virgin's Tomb, in the Kedron Valley below. Another name commonly used by the Arabs is *Bab el Asbat*, or "the Gate of the Tribes," from the "Birket Israel" or Pool of Israel, which is located just inside the gate and to the left as you enter.

Still another name is the Gate of the Lions, which is used by the Jews. This is derived from the two stone lions carved in relief on either side of the arch above the gate. The story regarding these lions is that Sultan Suleiman dreamed that he was being torn to pieces by four lions. The professional diviners were unable to interpret the dream satisfactorily, but a sheikh from a distant part, when called in, urged the Sultan to make a pilgrimage to Jerusalem. As a consequence, he determined to have the walls of the city rebuilt. The four stone lions are a memorial to the dream that led to the rebuilding of the walls.

St. Stephen's Gate is a square tower like the Jaffa Gate, but does not project beyond the outside wall. Its door is immediately before you as you enter the tower and you pass directly through into the city. As earlier noted, the principal street from this gate running westward entirely across the city is known for most of its way as the Via Dolorosa, or "The Way of Sorrows."

On a moonlit night, nineteen centuries ago, the Christ was arrested in Gethsemane, brought across the Brook Kedron and, many think, through St. Stephen's Gate, or its predecessor. He was then led bound to the palace of Caiaphas and the judgment hall of Pilate.

From its name, one would presume that this is a Christian gate. In a measure this is true, but it is even more   125

Herod's Gate

important to the Mohammedan, for it is the nearest open gate to the Temple area. It also leads to an important Mohammedan cemetery on the outside of the wall, some of the graves having large and picturesque domes. And it is through this gate that the long and colorful *Neby Musa* (Prophet Moses) procession used to enter the city on the annual trek from the supposed "Tomb of Moses" to the city of Jerusalem. This event usually coincided with the Jewish Passover and the Christians' Easter, and was one of the most colorful processions to be seen in the Holy City. St. Stephen's Gate was the gate-of-all-gates on this occasion.

It is a much used gate today, because it is the only gate that leads out of the city by the eastern wall, towards the Mount of Olives and the Bethany and Jericho roads.

The Eastern or Golden Gate

Of all the gates of Jerusalem, either closed or open, the Eastern Gate, or Golden Gate, is the most famous, the most significant, the most beautiful, and the most appreciated by the peoples of all races and creeds. It is now closed, but unlike the other closed gates, it continues to be exceedingly important.

Overlooking the Kedron Valley and facing the radiance of the rising sun and the Mount of Olives, this gate is located in the eastern wall, which at this point is also part of the Temple area enclosure. It occupies the middle of a slight projection 55 feet wide which extends outward six feet from the line of the main wall. It is a double portal spanned by two semicircular arches richly ornamented. From what resemble corbels, two Corinthian capitals project, sustaining an entablature which follows the outlines of the entire arch.

Over the gate is a magnificent gatehouse 55 feet square. The ceiling is divided into flattened domes, supported by arches which rest upon side pilasters, and from two Corinthian columns of polished marble, adorned with   127

St. Stephen's Gate

elegant capitals. Beneath the arches there is a pretty entablature carried from pilaster to pilaster, giving an air of exquisite beauty to the entire structure.

The Eastern Gate is unusually rich in names. Through its appearance, and through some confusion of name and place, it early became connected with the gate of the Temple known as the Beautiful Gate, where Peter and John met and healed the lame man who had asked them for alms. But this is in error, because "the gate called Beautiful" was a part of the main Temple structure—the principal or entrance gate leading directly into the Temple proper—rather than a gate of the eastern city wall which led into the Temple area. However, the two gates were near each other—the one leading into the Temple area, and the other leading into the inner Temple enclosure.

The Crusaders called it *Porta Aurea,* or the Golden Gate, and it is often so called at the present. The Arabic name for the entire gateway is *Bab ed Dahariveh,* which means "The Eternal Gate." But since it is a double gate, they call the north portal "The Gate of Repentance" *(Bab et Tobeh),* and the south portal "The Gate of Mercy" *("Bab er Rahmeh").*

The Eastern Gate has given rise to many contradictory theories in regard to its age, its builder, and the purpose for which it was erected. The present gate is a reconstruction of a gate of earlier date, and its foundations are even earlier. In fact, the walls and the gate in this area have not changed positions since the days of Jerusalem's ancient glory. Even Ezekiel, in his distant day, gave prophetic word concerning this well-known and highly revered portal. He spoke of it as "the gate whose prospect is toward the east" by which "the glory of the Lord" went up from the city, and by which, in vision, he saw it return (Ezek. 42:15; 43:4). He declared that the gate would eventually be closed, and gave the reason that it was to be reserved for the Prince of Peace, who had passed this way.

128

The closed, double-portaled Eastern or Golden Gate

Then he brought me back the way of the gate of the out-
ward sanctuary which looketh toward the east; and it was
shut.

Then said the Lord unto me; This gate shall be shut, it
shall not be opened, and no man shall enter in by it; because
the Lord, the God of Israel, hath entered in by it, therefore
it shall be shut.

It is for the prince; the prince, he shall sit in it to eat
bread before the Lord; he shall enter by the way of the porch
of that gate, and shall go out by the way of the same (Ezek.
44:1-3).

Approaching Herod's magnificent Temple from the
east, the people entered with considerable admiration
and pride by this gate. Through it Jesus Christ passed at
the time of His triumphal entry, while an enormous throng
spontaneously waved palm branches and shouted: "Hosanna to the son of David! Blessed is the King of Israel that
cometh in the name of the Lord." The Bordeaux Pilgrim of
A.D. 330, spoke of it as the Eastern Gate.

The present Golden Gate is a Byzantine structure
built by the Empress Eudoxia in the fifth century, and restored by Justinian or one of his followers about A.D. 560.
In A.D. 629 Emperor Heraclius, on coming back from con-
quering Chosroes, entered the city by this gate with what
was believed to be the Holy Cross. It seems that the Eastern Gate was then in a ruinous condition and Heraclius
took upon himself the responsibility of rebuilding it as a
memorial of (1) Christ's entry on Palm Sunday, and (2) his
own triumphal entrance after capturing and bringing back
what was considered to be the "true cross" of Christ.

In the year 810, for fear that a great Christian conqueror would enter this way, the Arabs closed the gate
and sealed it with solid masonry. Hereafter we have no
mention of its being opened until the Crusaders took possession of the place in 1102. At that time, Saewulf mentions it and says:

130   There is the gate of the city at the eastern part of the

temple which is called the "Golden Gate." . . . By the same gate the Lord Jesus, coming from Bethany on Palm Sunday entered the city . . . and by that same gate the Emperor Heraclius returned triumphant from Persia with the cross of our Lord.

The Crusaders reopened the gate and twice on each Palm Sunday the Patriarch, astride a donkey, led a procession through the gate. They provided this gate with wooden doors so that on other days it could be locked. But in 1187, when the Holy City reverted to the Arabs, the gate was walled up again, as it is today. The Christians could no longer perform their ceremonies there, but were obliged to enter the city through another gate. When Suleiman the Magnificent rebuilt the present walls in 1538-41, the Eastern Gate was freshly walled up and left much as it is today. As far as we know, it remained closed throughout the Turkish period—1514-1917.

The Arabs have a medieval prophecy to the effect that one day a great Christian conqueror will enter Jerusalem through this Eastern Gate. Many Mohammedans thoroughly believe that it will be Jesus Christ himself. Not until then, they say, will Jerusalem be really and finally conquered.

Thompson, after visiting the gate more than a hundred years ago, said, "My Moslem guide assured me that, 'at the end of the age,' Jesus, the son of Mary, would enter through that gateway, and take possession, not of Jerusalem only, but of the whole world."

The Dung Gate

The sixth open gate is the Dung Gate, which the Arabs sometimes call *Bab el-Mugharibeh*, or "the Gate of the Moors." It is a small, square entrance in the wall just large enough to allow men and beasts to pass in and out. It accommodates the street or roadway from the city through the Tyropoeon Valley, which lies between the Temple area   131

and the former Jewish quarters on the Western Hill. Being entirely destitute of architectural ornament, it is the most insignificant of all Jerusalem's gates.

The Dung Gate is Jerusalem's "back door," and as such, most of the refuse which comes from the city is taken out through this gate and used on the "King's Gardens" in the nearby Kedron Valley. From time immemorial, the sewer for the city seems to have run underground along the bed of the Tyropoeon Valley and out beneath the Dung Gate. Thus with fertilizer being carried out above ground and with the sewer underground it well-merited the name Dung Gate.

Nehemiah's city had a south gate by the same name, and this is presumed to be the modern representative of that ancient Dung Gate. However, the gate of Nehemiah's time was located much farther down in the Tyropoeon Valley.

Outside the gate, the roadway divides, one branch leading eastward to the Garden of Gethsemane, and the other southward past the Pool of Siloam, through the King's Gardens, and on to the village of Siloam.

The Zion Gate, or David's Gate

The seventh and last open gate of Jerusalem is the Zion Gate on the south. To the Arabs this gate is *Bab en-Neby Daoud,* or "Gate of the Prophet David," so named from its proximity to the Mosque of David, which is on the Western Hill.

Zion's Gate was built in A.D. 1541, as the inscription just above the doorway states, and at the same time as the remainder of the wall. The stones used in its construction are, for the most part, taken from earlier buildings. One of these stones bears a date comparable to A.D. 115 and records a victory of the Emperor Trajan.

The wall about the gate is higher than that on either side and is unusually massive. Within this wall is an orna-   133

The Dung Gate

mental arch of simple design, which, in turn, is so filled with dressed stones that there is space for only a moderate-sized, two-leaved door. Above the lintel of the door are two stones with their inscription in Arabic. Within the wall, on each side of the arch, are two vertical slits like loop-holes, and here and there a few rosettes and ornaments of carved stone. The gate is considered impressive because of its simplicity and its significant name.

Zion's Gate has long been used by the Christians, the Jews, and the Arabs who may have had occasion to go from the present walled enclosure of the city to that ancient portion of Jerusalem outside known as Zion's Hill, or the Western Hill.

Near Zion's Gate, within the city, has long been an open area provided and equipped by the Jewish women of America as a playgound for Jewish, Moslem, and Christian children. Outside the gate, on the Western Hill, is the place known as the Upper Room, and also the purported location of Christ's trial and Simon Peter's denial. Here, chiseled in stone, is the likeness of a man in the act of bitter weeping. It represents Simon Peter, who, after his denial, "went out, and wept bitterly."

GATES OF THE TEMPLE AREA

Of special interest to Mohammedans and to all who visit the Temple mount are the 11 gates which pierce the present north and west walls of the 35-acre Temple enclosure. Three of these gates are in the north Temple wall, and eight in the west wall. These, for the most part, are massive iron gates, 16 or more feet high, fitted into large stone portals. Only small iron doors, placed in these imposing larger gates, are kept open and then only at certain hours when outsiders are admitted to the Temple area for a fee and at the will of the guards.

Beginning on the east end of the north wall, there are 135

The Zion Gate

the Gate of Brothers, the Gate of Darkness, and the Enclave Gate.

On the western wall of the Temple court, beginning from the north, are: (1) the Gate of the Priests, (2) the Gate of the Judgment Court, (3) the Gate of the Painter, (4) the Iron Gate, (5) the Gate of Purity, (6) the Gate of the Cotton Merchants (the most beautiful of these gates), (7) the Gate of the Chain, and (8) the Gate of the Prophet, where legend says Mohammed tied his horse while he went to the Sacred Rock to pray.

THE CLOSED GATES

There are many other gates mentioned in the Bible which are not included in the above list. Most of these were destroyed with the walls of which they were a part. There are, however, a number of closed gates which may be seen in the lower portions of the present walls. The three most significant ones are: the Single Gate, the Triple Gate, and the Double Gate. They are all located in that imposing section of the south wall which encloses the southeast portion of the Temple area.

The Single Gate is the nearest of the three gateways to the corner. This closed entrance at one time led directly into the vaults of the Temple area now know as Solomon's Stables. Everyone who has inspected the masonry and construction of this gate regards it as a comparatively modern structure. Twenty feet beneath it, however, Captain Warren found an ancient entrance 12 to 18 feet high and 69 feet wide which he named the Great Passage. Lying as it does beneath one of the broad aisles of Solomon's Stables, we are led to believe this to have been in some way connected with the accommodation of horses. And according to Kings, Chronicles, Jeremiah, Nehemiah, and Josephus, the Horse Gate, which offered entrance to the kings' horses, was situated in the south wall near the southeast corner. This would place it at or near the present

The closed Triple Gate in the South Wall, leading into Solomon's Stables.

Single Gate. The presence of the Great Passage beneath the present gate would lead one to believe that such a position was quite probable. It was here that the wicked, unwanted Queen Athaliah was slain as she "rent her clothes" and ran from the Temple crying, "Treason, Treason."

> And he brought forth the king's son, and put the crown upon him, and gave him the testimony; and they made him king, and anointed him; and they clapped their hands, and said, God save the king.
>
> And when Athaliah heard the noise of the guard and of the people, she came to the people into the temple of the Lord.
>
> And when she looked, behold, the king stood by a pillar, as the manner was, and the princes and the trumpeters by the king, and all the people of the land rejoiced, and blew with trumpets: and Athaliah rent her clothes, and cried, Treason, Treason.
>
> But Jehoiada the priest commanded the captains of the hundreds, the officers of the host, and said unto them, Have her forth without the ranges: and him that followeth her kill with the sword. For the priest had said, Let her not be slain in the house of the Lord.
>
> And they laid hands on her; and she went by the way by the which the horses came into the king's house: and there was she slain.
>
> And Jehoiada made a covenant between the Lord and the king and the people, that they should be the Lord's people; between the king also and the people (II Kings 11:12-17).

The Triple Gate, sometimes called Huldah Gate II, lies near the halfway mark between the Single and the Double gates. It consists of three arched portals, each of which is 13 feet wide. These are closed with small masonry, but when they were open they gave access to three parallel passages which run a considerable distance under the Temple area, where they are now blocked with rubbish. There is also a passage up to the floor of the Temple area.

The original purpose of this Triple Gate can only be conjectured, but obviously it was an entrance of considerable importance, since three rather wide gates were placed side by side. There is the strong possibility that this Triple Gate was also used by the chariots and horses of the king to go in and out of the city. Action in time of war must needs be hurried, and this triple gate would expedite passage in such troublesome times. It would also be exceedingly commodious in times of peace.

The Double Gate is located 250 feet west of the Triple Gate, near where the present outer wall joins the Temple wall at the south side of the Mosque El Aksa. It corresponds to the Huldah Gate mentioned in the Talmud.

The gate consists of two arched entrances which show signs of having been constructed in the Herodian period, but which are now walled up with late Arab masonry. They formerly opened into a beautiful, four-domed vestibule measuring 30 by 40 feet. From the vestibule a fine, vaulted double passage ascends to the Temple grounds, reaching the surface near the principal entrance to the Mosque El Aksa. Through these passageways people came up from Ophel, and the lower levels, to the Temple Court on the summit.

The entrances are each 18 feet wide, and are separated by a large limestone column upon which rests the ends of great lintels which cover the gates. The arches are ornamented after the Byzantine style of architecture, and "form no part of the wall, but are simply fastened to it with metal clamps." Sir Charles Wilson, engineer to the Palestine Exploration Fund, says, "The Double Gate is undoubtedly a relic of the Temple of Herod." If Sir Charles is correct in this deduction, then it is quite probable that Herod, and also Christ, frequently entered the cloisters of the Temple by this passageway.

The Streets of the City

The old city of Jerusalem, enclosed within its walls and still completely Oriental in character, has three or four principal streets and many little, short streets or lanes. These are rarely more than 12 feet wide, are usually crowded, and always quaint to Western eyes. Some of the bazaars along the streets are vaulted, but most are open to the sun, so that as you walk along you constantly pass from strips of sunlight into bands of shadow. You mingle with all kinds of people, dressed in all kinds of clothing from all kinds of countries, who speak many kinds of languages. And as you walk, it is through history, with, as someone has put it, "an overpowering solemnity in the memory of all the Jerusalems that lie underfoot."

From Jaffa Gate, the people-packed David's Street, with its tiny, booth-like shops on either side, forms a continuous bazaar as it descends eastward in a series of stone steps. There are the food and vegetable stalls where one may purchase leeks, lentils, edible gourds, and other staple foods common since Bible times. Then there are the "shops" of the dry-goods merchants where one may purchase products ranging from the rich materials from the famous looms of Damascus and the East to the many "make-believes" straight from the factories of Europe. Just before it terminates at the Gate of the Chain, at the Temple area, there are so many money merchants that it is sometimes called the Street of the Money Changers. A short distance east of Jaffa Gate down David's Street, one turns to the left into Christian Street, which extends only to the Church of the Holy Sepulchre. Here one may purchase dry goods, notions, and a variety of souvenirs.

From Damascus Gate, an important street, which might properly be called "Center Street," traverses the entire city from north to south. Passing near the eastern side of the Church of the Holy Sepulchre, and on through the bazaars, it approaches the south wall, then sharply turns west and passes through Zion Gate. Another, named *El Wad* or Valley Street, branches off from near Damascus Gate and follows down the Tyropoeon Valley through the Dung Gate on the south.

From St. Stephen's Gate, a street goes westward, and with a couple of jogs passes through the New Gate. Much of this street makes up the world-famed Via Dolorosa, or "Way of Sorrows."

Each street, or a large section of that street, is set apart for a particular trade or craft, or as a marketplace or bazaar for the sale of certain commodities: the bakers have their street or quarter, as do the coppersmiths, the silversmiths, the tinsmiths, the money changers, the sellers of candles, cloth, clothing, tapestries, perfumes, spices, vegetables, sweetmeats, grain, and meats. There are also the sections for the makers of shoes, leather goods, mattresses, and all other necessities of Oriental life. The Valley of the Cheesemakers received its name from a street in the Tyropoeon Valley where lived many who carried on this craft.

CHAPTER 6

Historic Sites Surrounding Jerusalem

The natural features of the country surrounding Jerusalem remain substantially the same as in ancient times. The many hills and mountains mentioned in the Bible and ancient literature are there today, and form a ring almost around the city. These not only add to its picturesque beauty, but deepen its seclusion. They are as great outdoor stages upon which thrilling dramas have been enacted from time to time 142 during the past centuries, and they silently witness to these stories of adventure, both in grief and in gladness. The places of special interest around Jerusalem which thousands of pilgrims and tourists come every year to see are: *The Hill of Evil Counsel; The Potter's Field; Gihon, or The Virgin's Fountain; En-rogel, or Job's Well; The Mount of Offence; The Village of Siloam; The Mount of Olives; The Garden of Gethsemane; Chapel of St. Stephen; Tombs of the Kings; Solomon's Quarries; Jeremiah's Grotto; Golgotha (the "Place of the Skull").*

We will begin south of the Jaffa Gate, beyond the Valley of Hinnom, and proceed around Jerusalem in a counterclockwise direction.

The Hill of Evil Counsel

South of the Valley of Hinnom rises the traditional Hill of Evil Counsel, where stood the villa of Caiaphas. On an evil night, hostile high churchmen are said to have come here for counsel with Caiaphas, the high priest emeritus, concerning the most acceptable manner by which Jesus might be put to death. Here also Judas is said to have come "unto the chief priests," and told of his willingness to betray Christ, and to have bargained with them for 30 pieces of silver.

On the brow of the northern precipice of this hill, tradition alleges that Judas tied one end of a rope to an overhanging tree, and the other end of the rope about his neck. As he leaped off the precipice, the weight of his body broke the rope and he fell to his death in the deep, rocky bed of the Valley of Hinnom below. A lone tree now stands at this point and some pilgrims gaze on it with awe, holding the false notion that it is the very tree on which Judas hanged himself.

The Potter's Field

On the lower, cliff-like ledge of the eastern end of the Hill of Evil Counsel, a stone's throw south of the ancient 143 wall which surrounded Jerusalem in Christ's time, and 300 feet above where the Valley of Hinnom joins with the Valley of the Kedron, is located what is known as the Potter's Field. It is a rugged plot of ground in which is an artificially enlarged cave, vaulted over by a pointed arch and filled with enormous quantities of skeletons and moldering bones covered with the dust of ages. The badly deteriorated vaulting over the charnel house is partly of natural rock with the balance made up of masonry. Nine openings in the roof admitted the corpses as they were let down by ropes. Two caverns opened in the floor, from which numerous tunnels branched off into the hill, making room for tons of human bodies and bones.

Tradition designates this as *Aceldama,* or the "Field of Blood," which was purchased with the 30 pieces of silver returned by Judas Iscariot when he realized the enormity of his dastardly betrayal. "And they took counsel, and bought with them the potter's field, to bury strangers in. Wherefore that field was called The field of blood, unto this day" (Matt. 27:7-8).

St. Helena, Jerome, and other early pilgrims of the fourth century not only considered this as the Potter's Field which the chief priests purchased with the betrayal money, but they so used it in their day. The Crusaders also used it as a potter's field for the unclaimed bodies of pilgrims; and up to, and including, the last century, it was used for the same purpose. Today it is a ghastly sight, and the foul odors are so rank that they repel any who approach sufficiently near to make even a superficial survey of the place.

Gihon

This spring, now called The Virgin's Fountain, lies on the west side of the Valley of Kedron, not far from where ran the ancient Jebusite city wall, and just across the valley

Ancient steps in the street which leads down to the Pool of Siloam

from the village of Siloam. It was the chief source of water
for those who first founded Jerusalem, and the only living
spring known to exist in or near Jerusalem at the present
time. About it have centered many of the activities of the
city since its earliest beginnings.

The spring lies about 23 feet below the present
ground level, and is reached by a stairway of 33 steps. It
has a constant, though small, flow of water and also a very

strong intermittent flow. The name Gihon means "gusher," and was given to the spring because of its gushing forth periodically. During the winter months, when the rainfall is abundant, there are from three to four sudden, gushing flows per day. In the summer there are usually about two, and in autumn only one. During some very dry years, the autumn intermittent flow has been known to take place only once in three or four days. The normal flow of the spring during the winter season is about 250,-000 gallons a day.

To enable the early inhabitants of Jerusalem to secure water from the spring without going outside the city walls, the engineers chiseled a tunnel through the rock 36 feet west and 25 feet north, leading from the spring to a splendid basin which they had chiseled in the rock inside the city wall. The canal or tunnel had a slight fall so that the water from the spring could flow down to the rock-cut basin. The water was drawn up through a vertical shaft for use in the city. Captain Warren found an iron ring overhanging the shaft to which a rope had evidently been attached for drawing water. Some suppose that it was through this tunnel, or "gutter," that Joab reached the interior of the city to defeat the Jebusites and become David's chief and captain (II Sam. 5:6-8; I Chron. 11:6).

It was the water from Gihon Spring that King Hezekiah "stopped" from running outside the city and channeled through a 1,700-foot conduit bored under Ophel to the Pool of Siloam in another part of the city (II Chron. 32:30).

En-rogel

Known among the Arabs as Job's Well (*Bir Eyoub*), En-rogel is situated a few yards below the junction of the Kedron and Hinnom valleys. It was an important monument or point on the boundary line between Judah and Benjamin (Josh. 15:7).

Hezekiah's Tunnel, which conducts the waters from Gihon Spring to the Pool of Siloam.

The well is 125 feet deep and the water, which collects in a very large rock-hewn reservoir at the bottom of the well, is derived from the underground drainage of the three valleys. A certain amount of water flows down through the lower beds of limestone and naturally converges on this point.

There is water in the well all the year around, but during the rainy season, when occasionally there is constant rain for several days, the water sometimes rises above the well shaft and flows down the valley in a stream. This is considered such an event that many people come out from the city to see the sight.

It was here at the well En-rogel that Jonathan and Ahimaaz "stayed" during the initial stages of Absalom's rebellion, until a woman came from Jerusalem and told them Absalom's plans. Then, after a brief hiding, they went to David's encampment near the Jordan and informed him (II Sam. 15:27-28; 17:22).

It was by En-rogel that Adonijah, David's ambitious son, "slew sheep and oxen and fat cattle" and prepared a great feast for his adherents, and was abortively proclaimed king. Then he withdrew when he learned that Solomon was officially crowned king at the Spring Gihon, farther up the Kedron Valley (I Kings 1:5-49).

The Mount of Offence

Just across the Kedron Valley southward from the Temple area, is the Mount of Offence. It is, in fact, a southern spur of the Mount of Olives, and has been referred to as "the hill that is before Jerusalem." Here King Solomon erected pagan temples or "high places" for his heathen wives that they might worship their false gods— Ashtoreth, Chemosh, and Moloch—in the environs of Jerusalem (I Kings 11:7; II Kings 23:13). Hence its derogatory name. Milton, when speaking of this place where Moloch was worshipped, says:

> The wisest heart of Solomon he led
> By fraud, to build his temple right
> Against the temple of God, on that
> Opprobrious hill.

The present village of Silwan, site of the biblical Siloam

The Village of Siloam

This little village derives its name from the nearby Pool of Siloam, which is just west and north across the Kedron Valley. It consists of scattered houses, tier upon tier, on the lower northwestern ledges of the Mount of Offence. The rock cliff in the north portion of the village contains many tombs, some of which are extremely 149 ancient. At one time these caves were occupied by hermits. One was used as a chapel.

The place was immortalized by the incident in the preparation for the Triumphal Entry, where Jesus sent "two disciples" into Siloam—"the village over against you"—for a donkey, saying: "Ye shall find an ass tied, and a colt with her: loose them, and bring them unto me. And if any man say ought unto you, ye shall say, The Lord hath need of them" (Matt. 21:1-3).

The Mount of Olives

This historic mountain is called *Jebel et Tur* by the Arabs and is separated from Jerusalem by the deep and narrow Valley of the Kedron. It overtops the Temple hill of Moriah by 318 feet, and, rising to a height of 2,743 feet above sea level, is easily the most conspicuous landmark in the vicinity of the Holy City.

There has been an atmosphere of sacredness enveloping the mount from early times, and, aside from the Temple Mount, it has been the most revered and most constantly used mountain for religious purposes in Bible lands. Its very name is derived from the olives grown here, from which the oil was made for use in anointings and for other sacred purposes in the Temple.

It was sometimes called the Mount of Lights, because it was here, in ancient times, that the first official fire signals were lit to announce the first view of the new moon. This determined the happy event of the first Sabbath and thus the first day of the Jewish new year, and the beginning of each new month. At the first sighting, beacons were quickly lit on other faraway mountaintops until the chain of signals, first given on the Mount of Olives, had spread throughout the land.

Here on the Mount of Olives, the annual ritual offering for sin and uncleanness was carried out when the "red heifer" was brought "without the camp" to the top of the

Looking across the Kedron Valley towards Jerusalem from the Mount of Olives with the Dome of the Rock in the center.

mountain and there slain, burned, and her ashes sprinkled toward Jerusalem.

On the occasion of King David's fleeing from his rebellious son Absálom, he "went up by the ascent of mount Olivet," and came "to the top of the mount, where he worshipped God" (II Sam. 15:30, 32).

The Mount of Olives has always retained its essential feature, for during much of its recorded existence it has been fairly well clothed with olive trees. Some cypress, fig, mulberry, and other fruit trees also grow upon its slopes. As a favorite retreat and quiet resting place, it was very prominent in the life of Jesus. On its eastern slopes, in the village of Bethany, He made His home with Lazarus, Mary, and Martha. Here He spent many nights, returning in the morning to the Temple to teach the people, or at other times finding a quiet cave for meditation and prayer. How natural it was that "he sat upon the mount of Olives," over against the Temple, and with divine composure taught His disciples of prayer, of life, and of what should be "the sign" of His coming again, and of "the end of the world" (Matt. 24:3-14).

Once, as He came down from the summit, the full view of Jerusalem burst upon His vision, and in deep pity He wept over the city and foretold her fearful doom. Another morning, as He came along the southern slopes of Olivet, He saw a fig tree heavy with leaves. At His word it withered because there was no fruit, and no prospects of any—only leaves. Once He mounted a donkey and rode in triumph around the foot of the mountain toward Jerusalem while the people carpeted the way with their garments, waved palm branches, and shouted: "Hosanna; Blessed is he that cometh in the name of the Lord . . . Hosanna in the highest" (Mark 11:9-10).

On another occasion, when "every man went unto his own house," so the records inform us, "Jesus went unto the Mount of Olives" (John 7:53—8:1). And after the Last

Supper "he came out, and went, as he was wont, to the mount of Olives" (Luke 22:39). There He prayed until His betrayal.

From Olivet He ascended to heaven, while angels stood on the mount saying, "This same Jesus . . . shall so come in like manner as ye have seen him go into heaven" (Acts 1:11). And the prophet Zechariah, in speaking of Christ's coming to earth the second time, said: "And his feet shall stand in that day upon the mount of Olives, which is before Jerusalem on the east" (Zech. 14:4).

One could well wish that the mountain might have been left with its natural scenery so that its hallowed associations might be enjoyed to the fullest extent possible; but as it is now, the top of the mountain is covered with a loose cluster of buildings—churches, monasteries, mission houses, and hotels, along with many residences.

A short distance westward from the summit is the place where it is said Christ taught His disciples to pray. On the strength of this tradition, Empress Helena built a church here about A.D. 330. Peter the Hermit preached a mighty sermon here during the beginning of the Crusades, and the Crusaders erected another church here some years later. During the fifteenth century, St. Marks Church stood here but, like others, it deteriorated or was destroyed. The present beautiful building known as the Church of the Lord's Prayer was erected in 1868 by Princess La Tour d'Auvergne to perpetuate the tradition that it was here that Christ taught His disciples the Lord's Prayer.

On the walls of the colonnaded court of the church, the Lord's Prayer is engraved in 32 languages, on 32 marble slabs, each three feet wide and six feet long. Inside the church someone is in prayer constantly, and the Lord's Prayer is repeated often. Just in front of the church, on the south side, is a room with an iron, latticed door. Within is

Looking across the Temple Mount toward the Mount of Olives. Wailing Wall is in bottom center, Garden of Gethsemane in the valley beyond the Dome of the Rock, and the tower of the Russian Church of the Ascension at the top of the Mount.

the white marble tomb, and beautiful white marble statue of the princess who built and endowed the church.

On the central part of the summit stands the small, octagon-shaped Chapel of the Ascension, a relic of the roofless Church of the Ascension, erected in A.D. 375 with funds furnished by Emperor Constantine, and later restored by the Crusaders. It is said to be the oldest building on the mountain, which could possibly be true. Yet its location is hardly near enough to Bethany, nor does the chiseled-out "footprint of Jesus," inside the building, inspire any but the credulous. This building is now owned by the Moslems, but tourists are welcome, and the Christians conduct services there on certain days of the year.

The Tower of the Russian Church of the Ascension, on the eastern brow of the mountain, is a rather imposing structure, and from its top, one is afforded one of the world's most meaningful views. As one looks westward, Gethsemane and the Valley of the Kedron lie below, while opposite, spread out before you like a gigantic relief map, is the far-famed city of Jerusalem, with its walls, its turrets, its towers—and its Calvary. More has been accomplished in these environs for man's redemption than in any place on the face of the earth. To the south is Bethlehem, where the Christ Child was born and where came shepherds and the wise men.

To the eastward, there lies below the peaceful village of Bethany. Then on beyond you have a splendid view of the gray, desert hills of the Judean wilderness, the leaden-blue waters of the Dead Sea, and the high wall of the mauve-colored mountains of Moab which crowd the horizon beyond the sea.

To the north is Mount Scopus, on which is the German sanitarium (now used as the city hospital). It contains the throne room of the ex-kaiser, with a painting of him on the ceiling of the chapel. He is pictured enthroned amidst the crusading kings—Barbarossa, Richard the Lion-Heart, St. Louis, and others—as his equals. Next to him is a picture of Christ with His apostles.

Then, as the mountain ridge curves around to the west, there are the lower slopes of Mount Scopus on which Titus encamped during the A.D. 70 siege. The old Hebrew University, the original Hadassah Hospital, and the military cemetary entombing some 2,600 casualties of the First World War are located in this area. Somewhat farther northwestward is the ancient city of Nob, where stood the Tabernacle when David was a young patriot.

All the scenes viewed from the Russian Tower on the Mount of Olives are telescoped into such a small space— all within the range of the natural eye—yet of what in- 155 calculable worth to men are the events which took place here!

The Garden of Gethsemane

This historic "garden" was an extensive olive grove, with its oil press, which lay "over the brook Kedron" on the lower slopes of the Mount of Olives. It was opposite the Temple area, and was a secluded place where Jesus "often resorted with his disciples" (John 18:1), or went alone for quiet meditation. Here He agonized in prayer just before His final betrayal by Judas (Mark 14:32-50; Luke 22:39-54).

A tradition, dating from the early fourth century, places the garden about 50 yards east of the Kedron bridge. At this point there is now an enclosed area of about an acre which is very attractively laid out with winding paths and symmetrical beds of shrubs and beautiful flowers, a few tall cypresses, and eight gnarled olive trees. The latter are of extraordinary girth and of great age—so old in appearance as to make you almost believe the monks when they tell you that the trees grew here "in the time of our Lord." And with some the question does arise, Could the trees be quite so old?

Josephus states that Titus cut down all the trees around Jerusalem at the time of the siege in A.D. 70. This in all probability was true; yet olive trees, when cut, have a way of sprouting up from the stumps and continuing almost indefinitely. The sweet simplicity with which the garden is kept, and its quietness, make it a most impressive place for meditation. Millions visit the place and are deeply impressed by it.

A handsome basilica church, made entirely of Palestinian and Italian marble, and costing approximately $2 million, was completed here in the garden in 1926. Its front is Byzantine in style, and consists of a fine, three-arched portico with marble statues of the four Evangelists on Corinthian columns. Above these, on the pediment, is a brilliant mosaic of the Sermon on the Mount. Over the doorway, flanked by immense windows set behind white marble fretwork, is inscribed in Latin the Lord's request to His disciples: "Tarry ye here, and watch with me." Within the church, in the apse above the altar, is a fine mosaic depicting Jesus praying in the Garden: "Let this cup pass from me." The central portion of the floor of the church is beautifully paved with small, polished mosaics in scriptural designs, parts of which are survivors of the pavement of a fourth-century church, which the present has replaced.

A hundred yards eastward, and farther up the slopes of Olivet, is the Greek Orthodox site, which might well have been a part of the original garden. It too has its garden and trees, but its chief attraction is an ornate church built by Czar Alexander III in 1888. Its architectural design features a gorgeous roof with seven gilt, bulb-shaped domes, surmounted by Russian double-barred crosses towering above the dark green cypress and silvery olive trees of the enclosure. Now that there are no Russian pilgrims to worship in it and contribute to its upkeep, the site and the church have few visitors.

A quarter of a mile northward, along the mountainside, is a place farther away from the roadway which some think "more suitable and less artificial." However that may be, the olive garden where the Son of God agonized for man was somewhere in this area, and millions gladden to see a place which gives credence to the greatest concern ever recorded in the annals of history.

Chapel of St. Stephen

By the side of the Jericho road, near the junction with the road leading down from St. Stephen's Gate, is the Greek Orthodox Chapel of St. Stephen.

This simple and rather obscure building is said to mark the burial place of Stephen, the first martyr of the Christian Church. Not far away, in the direction of St. Stephen's Gate, is pointed out the spot where Stephen met his glorious death with the words, "Lord, lay not this sin to their charge." A young man whose name was Saul witnessed the stoning and he could not forget the occasion nor forgive himself until on the Damascus road the account was balanced with Christ.

Tombs of the Kings

A very fine tomb-complex, located about a half-mile north of Damascus Gate, is known as the Tombs of the Kings. Just how long it has carried this name we do not know, but in 1850 a Frenchman by the name of Felicien de Saulcy visited them and was told, in all good faith, that they were tombs of the preexilic kings of Judah. He so thoroughly believed the tradition that he boldly asserted that fragments, which he found, of a richly decorated sarcophagus lid belonged to the coffin of King David. In France his finds were received with considerable skepticism; therefore, in 1863, he obtained a Turkish permit for excavation, and returned to Jerusalem for more careful researches.

In his work of excavation, several beautiful sarcophagi were found, some of which were transported to Paris and placed in the Louvre. The most beautiful of these stone coffins bore the name of Queen Sadda inscribed in Aramaic. "Saada" was the Aramaic name of Queen Helena. (Helena is the Greek for "Sadda" as shown by the fragment of a clay vessel found in the coffin with the mark "Helen" in Hebrew letters.) This and other information led scholars to identify this tomb-complex as the mausoleum of Queen Helena of Adiabene (on the Tigris in Mesopotamia) and her descendants. She and her son
Izates were converted to Judaism during the first century

The heavy circular stone door at the entrance to the Tomb of the Kings

A.D., and she moved to Jerusalem. Josephus mentions that she and her royal son, Izates, were very liberal in dispensing relief to the Jews during a famine—presumably the one foretold by Agabus (Acts 11:28). Izates had 24 sons and many daughters. Seeing that this royal family used this unusually fine mausoleum, it was only natural for the people of Jerusalem to call it "the Tombs of the Kings."

This magnificent and extensive tomb-complex is regarded as the first and finest of the known tombs in or near the Holy City. On entering the gate, one descends a broad stairway leading into a small court. To the left a large doorway leads through a 12-foot-thick rock partition into an immense court 87 by 80 feet, the floor of which is 26 feet below the outside ground level. To the west of this are three stone steps and the beautifully ornamented entrance to the vestibule, which is 39 feet wide. The doorway to the tomb, somewhat below the level of the vestibule and to the left-hand side, is reached by two stone steps carved from the floor. The door itself consists of a very large and extremely heavy round stone which rests in a channel to the left of the open door. Two to four strong men must get down in this channel in order to roll the stone in front of the door to close it. Once there, it rests in a niche, which makes it most difficult to roll back. This gives essence to the words of the women on that Easter morn: "Who shall roll us away the stone from the door of the sepulchre?" (Mark 16:3)

The first room inside the tomb is about 18 feet square, and from it passages lead off to other rooms, which in their turn have passages to still other rooms—six rooms in all. All of these are cut out of marbled limestone. The walls and ceilings are so exactly square, and their angles so accurate, that no artisan with the most modern tools and instruments could have built them more regular. Except for the first, all of the rooms have funerary ledges or shelf tombs along the walls. These are sufficient to accommodate about 32 bodies when buried in regular style, but twice that number when crowded.

Solomon's Quarries

In 1852, Joseph Barclay was walking along the roadway parallel to the north wall of Jerusalem when his dog

Solomon's Quarries under the northern section of the Old City, where the white stones for the Temple were quarried and fitted.

disappeared in a cave-like opening under the wall about 300 feet east of the Damascus gate. Upon removing the debris he found that the passageway led into a large cave of stratified limestone. Deeper in the cavern a precipice was found marking the boundary of the main cave, which could be reached only by descending rude steps cut from the rock. At this point Barclay ignited a magnesium light and was deeply impressed by the labyrinth of subterranean quarries which were seen to run in three directions. The rocky pillars supporting the roof resembled the massive columns of a Norman cathedral whose naves and aisles ended in darkness.

The quarry extends southward under the city for nearly 700 feet. At some places the roof is quite low; in others it is so high that the light of candles is swallowed up in darkness. Here and there natural rock pillars have been left to support the roof, and in other places rocks have fallen from the roof. Occasionally one encounters dangerous pitfalls from which stones have been taken. The markings in the rocks along the side and end walls show the very shapes of large building stones removed by cutting a series of parallel grooves. These grooves were made with tempered copper tools, and wooden wedges were driven into them. When water-soaked, the wedges swelled and split away the large block of building stone. After the first stone was removed, it was an easier matter to remove the rest in the same tier.

All through the quarries are small shelves on which the ancients placed earthen lamps that gave light to the laborers. At the extreme south end there is a trickling, brackish stream, and on the ceiling not far away are the initials of certain leading men who have been there: "W. E. B." (for W. E. Blackstone), and others—all carefully inscribed by the black soot from burning candles.

The stone from this quarry is soft, white, and beautiful—the best in the vicinity. From the proximity of the quarry, the generous piles of dressing chips, and the quality of the stone, it is quite easy to believe that the stones were shaped and dressed here, then taken on sleds to the nearby Temple area, where the Temple was erected without the sound of a hammer or ax, "nor [was] any tool of iron heard in the house, while it was in building" (I Kings 6:7). Experts say that enough limestone has been taken from these quarries to build Jerusalem and the Temple of Solomon several times.

Jeremiah's Grotto

Outside the northern wall of Jerusalem, near Herod's Gate, is an ancient, natural cave or grotto which legend associates with Jeremiah. Tradition says that after Jerusalem was destroyed by the Chaldeans (Babylonians) in 586 B.C., and the greater part of the Jewish people carried away into captivity, Jeremiah sadly walked among the ruins of his beloved city, then retired to this cave and wrote the Book of Lamentations.

With his pen the piteous picture was built up of the deserted gates, the defiled Temple, the piled-up ruins, and the people who were led away captive.

> *How doth the city sit solitary,*
> *That was full of people!*
> *How is she become as a widow!*
> *She that was great among the nations! (Lam. 1:1)*

Then, in justification of God, he flings himself on the mercies of the Almighty:

> *Thou, O Lord, remainest for ever;*
> *Thy throne from generation to generation.*
> *Wherefore dost thou forget us for ever,*
> *And forsake us so long time?*
> *Turn thou us unto thee, O Lord,*
> *And we shall be turned;*
> *Renew our days as of old (5:19-21).*

163

Golgotha or Calvary

Both words, "Golgotha" derived from Aramaic, and "Calvary" from the Latin, mean "the skull" or "the place of the skull"; and refer to the place where Christ was crucified (Matt. 27:33; Luke 23:33). Whether it was called "the place of the skull" because it was a place of execution where skulls were found or because the site in some way resembled a skull is a matter of conjecture.

Many people witnessed the crucifixion of Christ, and there was a sufficient number who witnessed His burial to prevent any doubt at that time about the place. For about 37 to 40 years many people of Jerusalem knew well the place where He had been buried. Then came the tragedy of A.D. 70, when Titus destroyed the city. So complete was the destruction that no one lived there during the 60 years which followed. And it is doubtful if many of the former residents who were Christians ever lived there again. If so, then they were children when they fled from the city, and on their return would probably not have been able to identify places in their city where devastation had been so complete 60 years before.

The Scriptures merely indicate that the grim tragedy of the Crucifixion took place "near the city" (John 12:20) on a hill or an eminent place where it could be seen from a distance (Luke 23:49). A nearby roadway evidently passed through one of the city gates and on by the place of execution (Matt. 27:39). John states that the tomb was in a garden nearby (John 19:41).

Various sites have been suggested, but only two of these are seriously considered. One is the Church of the Holy Sepulchre, to which attention has already been given, and the other is Gordon's Calvary, with its Garden Tomb.

Gordon's Calvary is situated on a lone, gray hill north of Jerusalem, a "stone's throw" from the ancient wall, and about 700 feet outside the Damascus Gate. The site, which

(Above) Golgotha—"the place of the skull"—termed Gordon's Calvary, just a few hundred feet outside the Damascus Gate, now considered the probable place of the Crucifixion. (Below) The Garden Tomb at the base of Gordon's Calvary, where Christ is thought to have been buried.

covers three acres, may be seen plainly from every direction. As a hill it rises 40 to 50 feet above the surrounding terrain, and the side of the hill which is turned toward the city is rounded af the top and bears a "certain fantastic likeness" to a human skull. There are caverns for the eyes, a protruding rock for the nose, a long slit for the mouth, and a lower ledge for the chin—"quite as strong as is to be found in most of the nature resemblances which are commonly noticed in different parts of the world," says one writer.

In 1842, Otto Thenuis of Dresden studied this hill rather carefully and proposed that it was Golgotha. He pointed out that traditionally it was the Jewish place of stoning, that it lay outside the city, and that it showed the form of a skull. Then, one day in 1885, a famous Christian and British military man by the name of General Charles G. Gordon was out walking on the northern wall of Jerusalem. His attention was drawn to this skull-like, rock formation. On returning to the home of his friend, Horatio G. Spafford (writer of the song "It Is Well with My Soul," who then lived just inside the walls and later founded the American Colony), he said: *"Today I have found just the place for Calvary."*

General Gordon wrote to his sister and others about this possibility, then went on his way, and was killed three years later at Khartoum, Africa. Lew Wallace, Captain Conder, and others were inclined to agree with General Gordon's views. After a time, therefore, a portion of land west of the skull hill was purchased. During excavations, an ancient garden was found, and in it a tomb which had once been sealed by a rolling stone. Nearby excavations revealed other early Christian graves.

A company of English Protestants purchased the place, enclosed the area, and placed a guard at the tomb. After a time, the Protestant people decided that the guard was not needed. Today the nearby hill bearing the likeness of a skull is known as Gordon's Calvary, and the nearby garden, with its tomb, is known as The Garden Tomb. The latter is walled in, and just inside the gate is a neat home where lives a custodian who courteously shows visitors of all faiths the garden and the tomb.

The tomb is without ornamentation or ostentation, and for all that is the more impressive. No one worships the place, and it is to be hoped none ever will, but many notable Easter services have been conducted here. Moody and Talmage have been among those who have preached here, and hundreds of thousands have reverently gathered here from the four quarters of the earth. In a small measure they have felt the force and simplicity of the angel's words: "Come, see the place where the Lord lay" (Matt. 28:6).

Many excavations have been carried out, and efforts made to trace the course which the north wall must have taken during Christ's time. Herodian masonry underneath Damascus Gate indicates the presence of the wall in that area during Christ's time, but the exact course of the wall from Jaffa Gate to Damascus Gate must be traced before it can be decided if the site now occupied by the Church of the Holy Sepulchre was within or without the city wall. Until then, no final word may be given as to the exact site of Calvary or Golgotha. Nevertheless, the redemption made there remains effective still for those who believe.

The Jerusalem of Today

Jerusalem, like ancient Gaul, is of three parts: the Old City, the New Jewish City, and the New Arab City. These three make up greater Jerusalem—a city of some 275,000 people with no visible separation other than the medieval wall which encircles the oldest of the three. The place is administered by one government—the first time the Jewish people have ruled the Holy City for 1,900 years.

The *Old City*, with its narrow, dark streets, its closely packed roofs, its domes, its steeples, its minarets, its Temple grounds, its Wailing Wall, and its dense population, is, as of old, "a city that is compact together." Its people are chiefly Jews, Arabs, Christians, and Druses—each living pretty much in their own quarter, but mingling at intervals on a common basis as "the sons and daughters of Allah."

Its atmosphere, whether in home, street, workshop, or marketplace, is definitely Oriental—strangely akin to medieval towns and times. With little wheeled traffic, and an almost unbelievably heavy foot traffic, the people visit, browse, bargain, and take time to live a colorful and fascinating way of life that turns back the clock for many centuries.

The place is literally a "city builded upon her own heap," for beneath the level on which the people tread are the ruins of other previous Jerusalems—Crusader, Arabic, Byzantine, Roman, Greek, and Hebrew—each superimposed on the other.

The *New Jewish City* began in 1860, when Sir Moses Montefiore established the first Jewish settlement outside the walls, westward, near the old windmill. Later came ultraconservative Mea Shearim, and the quaintly attractive Bukharan groups. Then, with the Armistice of 1922, groups of Jews sitting on rock piles, cutting and squaring limestone building blocks, became one of the most common sights of this area. Architects, engineers, and expert town planners carefully plotted new districts and more Jews arrived in waves, as if some strange, superhuman force drew them "from all over the face of the whole earth."

So many of them wanted to settle only in Jerusalem that, to accommodate them, new districts had to be opened up. Brown, pink, and gray stone buildings—residential, commercial, religious, educational, admin-   169

istrative—multiplied into the thousands. What words can possibly describe the handsome new Kenesset (parliament) building, the new Hebrew University campus with its impressive National Library, the new Hadassah Hospital complete with nursing school and medical faculty buildings, the Biblical Zoo, and the Israeli Museum, with its fine archaeological wing, art pavilions, open-air sculpture garden, and the Shrine of the Book, which houses the Dead Sea Scrolls and other ancient manuscripts.

Few cities, if any, have so many really ultramodern, natural-stone structures. In such a setting 200,000 Jewish people reside and carry on the entire round of life. And few places have such a medley of life. Pressured by persecution and drawn by longings, these people have come from 70 different countries, speaking many languages, submerged in many cultures, possessing a variety of skin colors, yet all sharing the same feeling that they have "come home." The assimilation of these into one harmonious whole is only a little way beyond the beginning stage.

The *New Arab City*, usually referred to as East Jerusalem, has long had a few prominent buildings—religious, educational, and ancient family residences—most of which served more or less as landmarks. Following the division of 1948, however, the Arabs, and those who cast their lot with them, were left with no choice but to build their own Jerusalem east of "no-man's-land."

The concentration began north of Damascus and Herod's gates. Many new streets were laid out, extending far beyond the American Colony—even as far along the Ramalla Road as the hilltop site of ancient Nob. Arabs both of wealth and of moderate means caught the building urge and erected homes, hotels, low- and high-rise apartments, banks, cinemas, and even a YMCA building. Mammoth housing complexes developed—built here and there mostly of fresh-quarried limestone. The building area soon ex-   171

(Top) Israel's Parliament building, the Knesseth, situated on the heights of West Jerusalem. (Center) The Haddasah Medical Center on the western outskirts. (Bottom) The newer of two campuses of the Hebrew University.

tended eastward to Mount Scopus, to the Mount of Olives, and along both the Jericho and the Bethlehem roads. Even Arab sheikhs, whose families had lived in goat's-hair tents for long generations, have recently constructed beautiful, suburban homes, and live contendedly in them much of the year.

Jerusalem is the capital of a sovereign nation, a place of beauty, a center of learning and research, and the goal of pilgrims and tourists.

A Place of Beauty

"Beautiful for situation" was the exclamation of the Psalmist of old when he beheld Jerusalem perched high on its thousand-acre plateau and surrounded by its beautiful mountains. He knew, too, that true beauty had morality, goodness, and holiness as its constituent elements—that the Lord was in her and round about her to bequeath to her those unique qualities which would inspire the noblest human inspirations, and appeal to the whole earth.

And thus it is today, for Jerusalem is a city of natural grandeur on plateaus, on hills, and in valleys, with picturesque views of distant mountains, famous river courses, and mysterious seas. Its spiritual residue abounds in lingering memories and sacred influences of the Temple, the holy of holies, the ark of the covenant, the Garden of Gethsemane, Calvary, and the open tomb. Here a multitude of devout, selfless souls of the three major religions, who pray almost perpetually, have a vision of better things. They follow hard after God to bequeath to the place a moral and spiritual beauty which men have ever been fond of associating with Jerusalem, the "city of the great King."

A Center of Learning and Research

The Bible, along with the lands and people with which it has had to do, has evoked more interest and occasioned more study and research than all other literatures put together. And the yearning to return to Palestine and study the places where biblical characters lived is age-old. A new dimension was given to this about the middle of last century when improved topographical and excavational methods made it possible to locate and dig into the very city mounds where those people of the Bible had lived. To find the dishes from which they ate, the tools with which they worked, and the temples in which they worshiped thrilled a world waiting for more.

Many institutions for reasearch were established, and are now in Jerusalem: the Palestine Archaeological Museum, the Israel Museum, the American Schools of Oriental Research (now to be called "William Foxwell Albright School of Oriental Research"), the British School of Archaeology, the French School of Archaeology, the Hebrew Union College Archaeological School, the Israeli Exploration Society, the Hebrew University (with 12,000 students), and others. Israelis, Arabs, and scholars from many nations carry on excavations at various sites, and in most cases bring their "finds" to Jerusalem for interpretation, restoration, recording, and publication.

However, Jerusalem itself is the most important site for research. Topographical studies are constantly going forward, and here and there shafts are being sunk and trenches dug—at gates, beside walls, in the market areas, and at other strategic places. Ancient Jerusalem—now lying from five to 65 feet under the present city—is becoming better known each year.

A GOAL OF PILGRIMS AND TOURISTS

The long cherished, soul desire of seeing Jerusalem has caused millions through the ages to journey toward the Holy City. On hearing the cry, "Jerusalem," and gaining first sight of the city, they have been moved to tears by strange stirrings of the soul which have enriched life's 173 deeper meanings. Talmadge said, "After I have been ten thousand years in heaven, the memory of that first view from the rocks, on that afternoon of December second, will be as vivid as ever." Then he adds: "You see, it is a city unlike all others for topography, for history, for significance, for style of population, for waterworks, for ruins, for towers, for domes, for ramparts, for literature, for tragedies, for memorable birthplaces, for sepulchres, for conflagrations and famines, for victories and defeats."

With thoughts of the past and the future racing through the very soul, it is a common experience for one to enter through the gates of Jerusalem with the feeling, Here we are at last, in the true capital of the whole earth.

Literally millions of the finest people of our day are giving place to their long cherished desire to visit the Holy City, and in doing so are coming into those age-old inspirations—as deeply soul-moving as they have been in any generation. Jerusalem is, therefore, one of the world's foremost centers of pilgrimage, and tourism is the chief source of livelihood for those who live there. Hotels, boarding houses, low- and high-rise apartments, banks, tourist offices, buses, guides, souvenirs, and durable goods of various kinds to accommodate the pilgrims and tourists are being provided by those who anticipate their needs. They converge on Jerusalem every day, from almost every part of the globe—even Moslem pilgrims arrive from as far away as the Orient and Africa. One could almost believe that the urge to visit the Holy City is a universal desire—a prototype of that hope of going to the New Jerusalem which shall have no end.

Reference Notes

CHAPTER ONE

1. Ezek. 5:5.
2. I Kings 11:36.
3. Isa. 33:21.
4. Gen. 14:18, 20.
5. George L. Robinson, *The Bearing of Archaeology on the Old Testament* (New York: American Tract Society, 1941), p. 58; James B. Pritchard, *The Ancient Near East Texts* (Princeton, N.J.: Princeton University Press, 1958), pp. 262-74; Jack Finegan, *Light from the Ancient Past* (Princeton, N.J.: Princeton University Press, 1946), pp. 98-100.
6. Josh. 10:3-10.
7. The military maneuver made by David and his army, and especially that of Joab, is fairly easy to follow in the present topography of Jerusalem.
8. II Chron. 12:9.
9. Martin Knott, *Students' History of the Hebrews* (no data), p. 231.
10. G. Frederick Owen, *Abraham to Allenby* (Grand Rapids, Mich.: Wm. B. Eerdmans Publishing Co., 1939), p. 86.
11. II Kings 19:33-36; II Chron. 32:21.
12. Luke 2:1-16; Matt. 2:1-6.
13. Flavius Josephus, "Wars of the Jews," *The Works of Flavius Josephus* (Philadelphia: David McKay Publishers, n.d.), Book V, p. 804.
14. Michel Join-Lambert, *Jerusalem* (New York: Frederick Ungar Publishing Co., 1958), p. 105.
15. If the present "Tower of David" was Pilate's "Praetorium" or his palace where he pronounced judgment on Christ, then it has been suggested that General Allenby's proclamation of peace may well have been given near the same place.
16. Luke 21:24.

CHAPTER TWO

1. The city's name in Hebrew—Yerusalayim—has the dual ending which could conceivably refer to the "upper" and the "lower" cities so often mentioned in history.
2. Ps. 125:2.
3. II Sam. 18:18.
4. Josh. 15:8.
5. Jer. 6:1.
6. II Kings 23:10.
7. I Kings 10:5.

CHAPTER THREE

1. I Chron. 11:7-8.
2. I Chron. 11:4-9.
3. I Kings 2:10.

4. Neh. 3:15-16.

5. Acts 2:29.

6. G. Frederick Owen, *Archaeology and the Bible* (New York: Fleming H. Revell Co., 1961), p. 80.

7. Kathleen M. Kenyon, *Jerusalem: Excavating 3000 Years of History* (New York: McGraw-Hill, 1967), pp. 14-53.

8. II Chron. 32:30; II Kings 20:20.

9. Also see Pritchard, *op. cit.*, p. 212; Kenyon, *op. cit.*, p. 70.

10. John 9:7.

11. Deut. 12:10-14.

12. II Sam. 24:16-25.

13. I Chron. 21:25.

14. I Chron. 22:1.

15. I Chron. 28:2-21.

16. II Chron. 7:13-46.

17. I Kings 8:6; II Chron. 5:7.

18. The dimensions and descriptions of the Temple are found in the Old and New Testaments, in Josephus, in the letter of Aristeas, and in the Middoth (a section of the *Mishna*). See Mid., 11, 6: Vol. I.

19. Josephus, *op. cit.*, Book V, 5:3.

20. Acts 3:1-10.

21. Luke 21:1-3.

22. Josephus, *op. cit.*, "Antiquities." Book VIII, 3:2; Book XV, 11:3. That David gave to Solomon the pattern of the Temple which had been prepared by him under direct supernatural direction can be objected to only by those who deny the possibility of such divine communications and revelations being made by God to man. In Middoth 4:7 it is stated that Herod, in his attempt to build according to the plan used by Solomon, extended the porch 15 cubits (22½ feet) wider on each side—45 feet wider in all. This made the Temple "narrow behind and wide in front—like a lion."

23. Exod. 28:29-36.

24. *Cherubim.* Some have said the pattern of the cherubim in the holy of holies was borrowed from Phoenicia, but this is without basis in fact. The winged, sphinxlike, mythological creatures of Syrophoenicia had sexy animal bodies, human heads, abnormally large noses, short wings, and harmonized with the materialistic, sensual religion of the Syrophoenicians. They flanked the throne chair of King Hiram of Phoenicia, and adorned the bedstead and bedroom ceiling of the Ahab-Jezebel palace at Samaria.

But *never*, at any time, nor at any place, in archaeological research has anything been found that even intimates that any of these imaginary creatures had any connection with or anything whatever in common with the cherubim, or heavenly guardians that stood at attention, with their long wings outstretched above the mercy seat—the very footstool of God—in the holy of holies in the Temple at Jerusalem.

Furthermore, the winged sphinx and other such creatures were represented as crouched, or rising doglike on their all-fours with their short wings bent backwards, while the cherubim in the holy of holies stood at attention with their long, outstretched wings covering the sacred ark, the mercy seat, and the entire span of the holy of holies. Ezekiel says plainly of the cherubim he saw: "This was their appearance; they had the likeness of a man" (Ezek.

176

1:5)—just as angels have always been made to appear, and as one at Nimrud appeared.

The religion of Israel, in its pure form, was *divinely spiritual*. And the records tell us that God Almighty—absolute in power, in holiness, love, and justice—designed the ark and the mercy seat, and the "two cherubims of gold" who should "stretch forth their wings on high, covering the mercy seat with their wings." God charged Moses plainly, "And look that thou make them after their pattern, which was shewed thee in the mount" (Exod. 25:10-22, 40). And the similar plan for the larger cherubim in the holy of holies of the Temple at Jerusalem was likewise given to David by the Lord (I Chron. 28:11-12, 19).

The religion of Israel as revealed by the Lord was on such an infinitely higher moral and spiritual plane than the heathen religions about them that there was no need whatever for their "borrowing" from neighboring peoples and countries. And there is no good purpose to be served by saying that Israel, who was to be a "separate" people, was at this time on a long drift from God, and for this reason were influenced by paganism around them. The facts are plainly stated that both the Tabernacle and the Temple, and the arrangements for their services, were *from God* and not from the people. God *revealed* the plan to show the people the *way to God*—step by step through the Temple to God in the holy of holies under the wings of the "holy cherubims." These steps of repentance, prayer, and consecration were later to be more clearly revealed by the prophets and by Jesus Christ.

25. Isa. 6:1-3.
26. Exod. 23:20.
27. Matt. 27:51; Mark 15:38.
28. Macc. 2:4-7.
29. Josephus, *op. cit.*, "Antiquities." XV:40. The "altitude" of the Temple, referred to by Herod, was the 180 feet which both the Bible and Josephus give. Herod built the Temple 150 feet high. Josephus speaks of a 30-foot extension which he added on top of the 150 feet, making it the 180 feet. This last 30 feet could well have been the "pinnacles."
30. Luke 4:9. Jesus was on "a pinnacle of the temple" rather than on a tower of the southeast wall, as some have suggested.
31. John 2:20.
32. Luke 2:46.
33. Matt. 4:5-6.
34. Mark 13:1-2.
35. Josephus, *op. cit.*, "Wars," Book V, 4:1.
36. Mr. J. Nussibeh, a friend and former classmate, is the official keeper of the Church of the Holy Sepulchre, and has made a large contribution to my understanding of the church. It is a high privilege to go through the church under his supervision.
37. Josephus, *op. cit.*, "Wars," Book V, 4:2.
38. Acts 21:40.

CHAPTER FOUR

1. II Sam. 5:6-9.
2. I Kings 9:15.
3. Neh. 4:17.

4. While the very stones in a wall are a study in archaeology, yet the types and styles of masonry cannot *always* be relied upon to precisely date a wall. Furthermore, dating criteria such as pottery, coins, and other artifacts do sometimes get misplaced or mixed up where debris has been disturbed by earthquakes, churned by winter torrents, or moved and mixed by other factors.

5. E. Robinson and E. Smith, *Biblical Researches in Palestine*, "Mount Sinai and Arabia Petrea" (Boston: Crocker and Brewster, 1841), Vol. I.

6. Sir Charles Warren, *The Recovery of Jerusalem* (New York: D. Appleton and Co., 1871), p. 95.

7. *Ibid.*, p. 98.

8. *Ibid.*

9. *Ibid.*, pp. 107-18.

10. *Ibid.*, pp. 226-27.

11. Kenyon, *op. cit.*, pp. 22-24.

12. For a further discussion of this problem, see Wright and Filson, *The Westminster Historical Atlas of the Bible* (Philadelphia: The Westminster Press, 1956), p. 99.

13. Josephus, *op. cit.*, "Wars," Book V, 4:3.

14. Chester C. McCown, *The Ladder of Progress in Palestine* (New York: Harper and Brothers, 1943), p. 236.

15. For a careful discussion of these excavations, see *Bulletin* of the American Schools of Oriental Research, No. 89 (Feb., 1943), pp. 18-21.

16. Excavations reveal wall remnants below the present structure which are older.

17. Josephus, *op. cit.*, "Antiquities," Book XV, 9:3.

18. Josephus, *op. cit.* "Wars," Book V, 4:1.

19. Rabbi Benjamine of Tuedela, who traveled through the holy lands as far back as 1167, referred to the Western Wall as the Gate of Mercy.

20. Teddy Kollek and Moshe Pearlman, *Jerusalem, a History of Forty Centuries* (New York: London House, 1968), p. 268.

21. *Ibid.*, p. 269.

CHAPTER FIVE

1. Ezek. 48:30-35; Rev. 21:12-13, 21.

2. Deut. 3:5; Judg. 16:3; Neh. 3:6.

3. Josh. 2:5-7; Neh. 3:19.

4. Gen. 23:10-18.

Bibliography

Burrows, M. "Jerusalem," *The Interpreter's Dictionary of the Bible*. New York: The Arlington Press, 1962.

Cornfeld, Goodyolin. *Pictorial Bible Encyclopedia*. New York: The Macmillan Company, 1964.

Edersheim, Alfred. *The Temple*. Grand Rapids, Mich.: Wm. B. Eerdmans Publishing Co., 1950.

Eversull, Harry K. *The Temples of Jerusalem*. Cincinnati: Masonic Memorial Chapel Association, 1946.

Glueck, Nelson. *The River Jordan*. Philadelphia: The Westminster Press, 1946.

Join-Lambert, Michel. *Jerusalem*. New York: Frederick Ungar Publishing Company, 1958.

Josephus, Flavius. *The Works of Flavius Josephus*. Philadelphia: David McKay Publishers, n.d.

Kenyon, Kathleen M. *Jerusalem: Excavating 3,000 Years of History*. New York: McGraw-Hill Publishing Co., 1967.

Knight, William. *The Arch of Titus and the Spoils of the Temple*. London: Religious Tract Society, 1896.

Kollek, Teddy, and Pearlman, Moshe. *Jerusalem, a History of Forty Centuries*. New York: London House, 1968.

McCown, Chester C. *The Ladder of Progress in Palestine*. New York: Harper and Brothers, 1943.

McGarvey, J. W. *Lands of the Bible*. Philadelphia: Lippincott Company, 1882.

Mayor, Benjamin. *The World of the Bible*, 5 vols. New York: McGraw-Hill Book Company, 1958.

Owen, G. Frederick. *Abraham to Allenby*. Grand Rapids, Mich.: Wm. B. Erdmans Publishing Co., 1939.

————. *Archaeology and the Bible*. New York: Fleming H. Revell Co., 1961.

Palestine Exploration Fund Quarterly Statement for 1886. London: Office of the Palestine Exploration Fund.

Parrot, Andre. *The Temple of Jerusalem*. New York: Philosophical Library, 1955.

Paton, L. B. *Jerusalem in Bible Times*. Chicago: University of Chicago Press, 1908.

Payne, M. A. "Jerusalem," *The New Bible Dictionary*. Grand Rapids, Mich.: Wm. B. Eerdmans Publishing Co., 1962.

Petrie, W. Flinders. *Six Temples at Thebes*. London: Bermaid Quaritch, 1897.

Pritchard, James B. *The Ancient Near East Texts*. Princeton, N.J.: Princeton University Press, 1958.

Robinson, E. *Bible Encyclopedia*. Toledo, Ohio: H. W. Snow and Company, 1881.

Robinson, George L. *The Bearing of Archaeology on the Old Testament*. New York: American Tract Society, 1941.

Robinson, E., and Smith, E. *Biblical Researches in Palestine*, 3 vols. Boston: Crocker and Brewster, 1841.

Rosenthal, Gabriella. *Jerusalem*. New York: Doubleday and Company, 1968.

Schmidt, Emanuel. *Solomon's Temple*. Chicago: University of Chicago Press, 1902.

Steckool, S. H. *The Gates of Jerusalem*. New York: Frederick A. Praeger Publishing Co., 1968.

Wallace, Edwin Sherman. *Jerusalem the Holy*. New York: Fleming H. Revell, 1898.

Warren, Sir Charles. *The Recovery of Jerusalem*. New York: D. Appleton and Company, 1871.

Wilson, Col. R. E. *Picturesque Palestine*, 2 vols. New York: D. Appleton and Company, 1881.

Wright, G. Ernest, and Filson, Floyd V. *The Westminster Historical Atlas of the Bible*. Philadelphia: The Westminster Press, 1945.